SECRET SHOP WEAPONS

SECRET SHOP WEAPONS

Jewelers Reveal Their Favorite Tools—
and Why They Love Them

Technical Editors: Ann Cahoon & Chris Ploof

MJSA PRESS
Professional Excellence in Jewelry Making & Design

MJSA would like to thank the prime sponsor of *Secret Shop Weapons*, Rio Grande.

©2012 MJSA
ISBN 978-0-9799962-1-4
Library of Congress Control Number: 2012936340

Published by MJSA Press, 57 John L. Dietsch Square, Attleboro Falls, MA 02763; 1-800-444-6572 (U.S. only) or 1-401-274-3840; e-mail *info@mjsa.org*; *www.mjsa.org*.

A portion of the articles in this book originally appeared in modified form in *MJSA Journal*. *MJSA Journal* is published monthly by MJSA. For information about subscribing to *MJSA Journal*, call 1-800-444-6572 (in U.S. and Canada only) or 1-401-274-3840; fax 401-274-0265; e-mail *info@mjsa.org*; *www.mjsa.org*.

Photo Credits: Cover photos courtesy of (l-r) Alan Revere, Mark Maxwell, and Gary Dawson. All photos provided by the artists featured except for the following: Todd Pritchett (head shot, page 12); Copyright by Carl Zeiss (page 17); Travis Searle (pages 24, 26, 88 [tool shot], 90, 118-143); Rio Grande (pages 8, 25, 76, 83, 86, 89, 97); LaserStar Technologies (laser, page 39); Betty Helen Longhi (brake photo, page 44); Lydia Tutunjian (head shot, page 56); Matt Yegge (page 56); Adrienne Krieger (head shot, page 62); Edwin Ross (pages 62, 63); Glendo/GRS (page 73); Simon Martin (head shot, page 74); Lenovo (page 75); Pat Jarrett (head shot, page 86); Randy Reynolds (page 87); Anne Staveley (page 92); Craig Pratt (pages 93, 94); Dawn Temple, Bellaria Design (pages 98, 99); Marilyn O'Hara (pages 110, 111); NC Black Co. (tools, page 111); Richard Duane (page 113); and Alexa Nesal (page 114).

Safety Notice: The contents of this book are solely the work of the authors and have not been tested or authorized by MJSA, *MJSA Journal*, or MJSA Press. The use or application of information, practices, and/or techniques pertaining to jewelry manufacturing, jewelry repair, or other related topics in this book may be hazardous to persons and property, and they are undertaken at the reader's own risk.

Book design by Jesse Snyder, Stout Graphics. *stoutgraphics.com*

Table of Contents

---------------- *CONT.* ----------------

Table of Contents (cont.)

Subj:

OPERATION
SECRET SHOP WEAPONS

It's no secret that jewelers love their ███████ tools. Even the tools
that are messy, loud, or a bit of an ordeal to use, because at the end
of the day they all help to get the job done. But every jeweler has a
soft spot for one special tool. The tool that makes their job both a
little bit easier and a lot more fun. ████████████████████████
The one tool that they couldn't imagine ever being without. It is, if
you will, their secret shop weapon.

Now, for your eyes only, more than 30 jewelers confess and reveal
their secret shop weapons—what they are, what feats they allow
them to overcome, and why they love them so. ████████████████
It doesn't matter if it's a $15K technological wonder or a $2 bar-
gain bin find; these are the tools that allow their owners to declare
"mission accomplished."

Your mission, if you choose to accept it, is to read about these secret shop weapons and the discoveries the jewelers have made
with them. Then take a look around your own shop and see how
many of these weapons you possess. Are you using them to their
maximum potential? Also, think about which of your tools is *your*
secret shop weapon. ████████████████████████ What tool
helps you accomplish the near impossible? What new discoveries
await you and your beloved tool?

Finally, keep this book secure in a ███████████████████████ top-
secret location. While it won't self-destruct once you finish read-
ing it, the book could still disappear, becoming someone else's secret shop weapon.

*[Note: No torture was used to obtain the intelligence in these pages.
The editors observed all protocols under the Geneva Conventions
while gathering this intel.]*

REGSTR\\DOC SER#032012

SHOP TIPS FOR
SAFE PRACTICES

One of the best "secret shop weapons" any jeweler can have is a respect for shop safety. Below are a few basic practices that should always be followed.

• Wear eye protection when performing any task at the bench. With some operations, the need is obvious, such as when metal chips are flying from a drill bit. But all operations have their hazards: Hammer heads can fly off, files can break, and saw blades can snap, creating projectiles that could blind you. Some jewelers take an additional step and wear a face shield. As one noted: "I have a scar on my cornea from a metal splinter that got past my safety glasses." To ensure easy access, buy several pairs of glasses or face shields and place them at every workstation.

• All torches using pressurized fuel gas and oxygen must have flashback arrestors installed on either the handle of

> Wear eye protection when performing any task at the bench.

the torch or the regulator. The arrestors must be approved by Underwriters Laboratory (UL). Keep cylinders of compressed gas chained. If you install a fixed gas supply, hire trained, licensed professionals to perform the installation (or at least to provide guidance). If you use low-pressure utility natural gas, boosting the oxygen pressure to compensate will increase the potential for a dangerous torch flashback. Use a natural-gas torch booster instead.

• Ventilate to remove the plume of smoke or fumes caused by soldering.

<9>

• Butane lighters can be handy to strike torches, but should never be left near the bench if they have fuel left in them. Better to stick to the strikers intended for the job.

• To avoid splashes and mists, do not quench metal in pickle. Quench in water. (Note: A sodium bisulfate pickle is preferable to sulfuric acid. Citric acid is also more "jeweler friendly.")

• Every time you use a hammer, make sure its head fits tightly. Make sure any chasing tools are properly tempered so they won't snap.

• When using a flex-shaft, do not use a tool that is too long or heavy for the chuck; it could suddenly bend to a right angle and become a fearsome propeller. Never use a drill or accessory that appears to be wobbling, out of round, vibrating, or not running true.

• When using a flex-shaft or polishing equipment, never wear dangling jewelry or loose clothing that could become caught in the equipment. Tie long hair back.

• Place a soft pad below the polishing buff to prevent items caught on the wheel from bouncing back at you.

• Dust masks (or respirators, for toxic metals and materials) should always be worn when polishing or grinding. Also, install a dust collection system that is appropriate for the metals and abrasives used, and clean it regularly.

• Employ good lighting: It avoids eyestrain and helps you to perform better.

• Perform regular maintenance on your tools and equipment.

• Keep a handbook that identifies the chemicals you have in your shop. Include in it the Material Safety Data Sheet (MSDS) for each one, along with step-by-step emergency plans and local police, fire, and rescue contact information. Keep chemicals in tightly closed, unbreakable containers, and label them clearly.

• Store only the chemicals you need, and have just enough on hand to last several months.

• Keep a first-aid kit on hand; make sure it's fully stocked and easily accessible.

The above tips are adapted from "The Safe Bench" and "Chemical Safety" by Charles Lewton-Brain, which appeared in the MJSA publication Safety Solutions.

<11>

Secret Shop Weapons

On the following pages, more than 30 jewelers and designers reveal the tools they just can't live without. They also describe why they love their "secret weapons"—what advantages the tools provide, as well as some of the discoveries and breakthroughs that they've helped to achieve. An assortment of "Secret Shop Tips" rounds out this section.

Subj:

WHY BELLE BROOKE BARER LOVES HER...
MINI-BURNISHER

SO TELL US. WHAT'S YOUR SECRET WEAPON?

The mini-burnisher for the flex-shaft. I make my own, and it's really effective—I take a steel mandrel from an old rubber polishing wheel, anneal it, bend it, and then do whatever I want with it.

WHAT DOES IT DO?

It erases tool marks and smooths

seams and pits. You can also use it to fix a stamp mark that did not go the way that you anticipated. I use it as part of the preliminary cleanup for any piece I've fabricated.

WHY DO YOU LOVE IT SO MUCH?

Sometimes, after a final polish is ap-plied, you notice there are some areas that were not cleanly soldered or have tool marks. Especially at that stage, you don't want to have to go in with heat to fix the problem. Also, bringing a piece under a torch too many times can compromise the joints, especially if you're working with silver (as I mostly do). If the damage isn't a major problem, using a mini-burnisher saves so much time; the problem can be corrected quickly and with ease. Also, it is a great go-to for refurbishing a piece (usually a ring) that a customer has "worn hard," so to speak.

WHAT DOES IT ENABLE YOU TO DO THAT NO OTHER TOOL DOES?

It moves metal without removing it.

<13>

You may not want the size or shape of something to change, and the mini-burnisher keeps that from happening.

WHAT DISCOVERIES OR BREAKTHROUGHS HAVE YOU MADE WITH THIS TOOL?

It has really helped me to develop an attention to detail. I was first introduced to it at my bench job when I was fresh out of my jewelry training, and everyone who has worked for me has gushed about how amazing it is and how happy they are to have learned about it—it's amazing how much a little piece of steel can do. There's really no excuse for sloppy finishing if a jeweler has one of these.

<15>

REGSTR\\DOC SER#032012

SECRET SHOP TIPS

Burnish Your Image

One of the oldest forms of polishing, burnishing still has an important place in contemporary jewelry making. Burnishing was once the main way to make metal shine. Today it is used to highlight the edges of pieces, to detail areas of stone settings, and as an alternative to polishing.

Burnishing involves rubbing a metal surface with a harder, smoother, polished material. This process smears and flows the surface, brightening it and filling porosity. Jewelers' burnishers are usually made from steel, gemstone (agate or hematite), and sometimes tungsten. To locate or make the best burnisher for your needs and use it effectively, check out the following tips:

• To find your own gemstone burnisher, hunt around rock and crystal shops. Most will have a box of tumbled agates. Look for an agate with a long, tapered shape or a round shape that has a hook to it (the hook is very useful for burnishing the edges of sheet metal). You can also cut specific grooved shapes into the stone using silicon carbide separating discs (use moisture to avoid dust) and gem polishing pastes. Or ask a hobby lapidary to turn out a particular shape for you.

• Steel burnishers can likewise be altered for different jobs. For example, to burnish edges, you can add a polished groove.

<<By Charles Lewton-Brain>>

Balancing Act

Since they are typically used at moderate to high speeds, rotary burnishers made from annealed and bent burs tend to vibrate if they aren't balanced. This vibration, besides causing hand fatigue and tingling in the fingers, also makes the tool harder to use precisely. For a more balanced approach, take a worn-out round or wheel bur, custom-grind facets on the face (anything from four facets on up is possible), and apply a final polish. As long as you grind evenly and keep the bur cool (so the temper won't be affected), you will have a burnisher that runs better at higher speeds, without hand-numbing vibrations.

<<By Chris Ploof>>

CLASSIFIED

Subj:

WHY JIM BINNION LOVES HIS... ZEISS BINOCULAR LOUPES

SO TELL US. WHAT'S YOUR SECRET WEAPON?

Zeiss binocular loupes.

HOW DO YOU USE THEM IN YOUR WORK?

I wear them at the polishing motor. I wear them at the lathe while cutting patterns. I wear them doing almost anything at the bench. They're like a set of bifocals; I can look over the top [of them] and see stuff across the shop, but drop my eyes down and look at something with 4x magnification.

WHY DO YOU LOVE THEM SO MUCH?

In 1999, a couple of years after I started doing [jewelry making] full time as a profession, my back was killing me. I was using an Optivisor, and to see the work, I had to sit hunched over my bench. I would spend hours in that hunched position, and it wasn't great. Then I saw a mention of the Zeiss loupes on the Orchid e-mail forum [run by the Ganoksin Project, *ganoksin.com*]. I called the Zeiss representative and she sent me two sets to try out. I picked out a set that has a

4x magnification at 300 millimeters, and all of a sudden it was like I was wearing a #10 Optivisor, but I could sit up straight at the bench.

WHAT DO THEY ENABLE YOU TO DO THAT NO OTHER TOOL DOES?

They allow me to see what's happening down at the point where the tools are cutting the metal. I would be lost without those things.

WHAT DISCOVERIES OR BREAKTHROUGHS HAVE YOU MADE WITH THEM?

Overall, they've allowed me to work at a higher level. Being able to clearly see each step of the process, to be

<17>

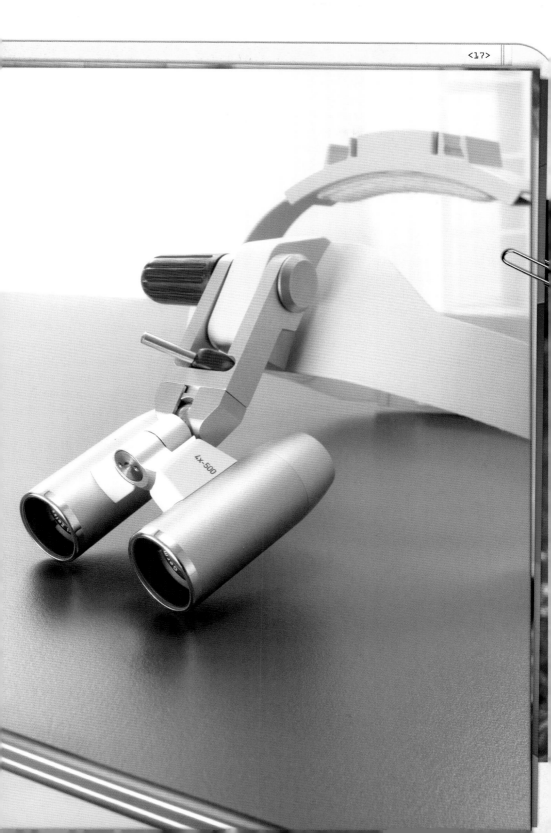

certain I like how a job is progressing and be able to react sooner to problems, has made a huge difference in my work. And because I'm looking at such a fine level of detail, I know that if I'm happy with the way a piece looks at 4x magnification, it should look fine to the naked eye. I literally wear the things all day long, because one of the biggest lessons I've learned is, If you can't see it, you can't do it.

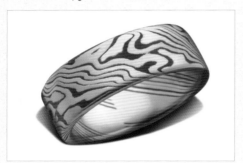

<19>

SECRET SHOP TIPS

All Wrapped Up

It's best not to rub a wax or finished piece of jewelry on a wooden bench pin imbedded with metal filings. Instead, use a spare bench pin covered with bubble-foam wrap—its cushiony surface is ideal for finishing up waxes, and it's also handy for final touch-ups on polished metal pieces. To create your own, wrap a bench pin with double-stick tape, leaving some tape hanging off the end of the pin. (Although double-stick carpet tape is best, other tapes, such as cellophane, work well, too.) Now wrap the pin in bubble foam and trim to fit; the extra strip of tape will secure it tightly. After cutting out the V at the end of the pin, put more tape in the seam.

You can also make bench pins wrapped with soft cotton cloth, moleskin (flannel with adhesive on the back—it can be found in drugstores), and rubber (provides a great no-slip grip). The sky's the limit! Try something new—Astroturf, anyone?

<< By Kate Wolf >>

Shedding Some Light

David Winnie of F&J Manufacturing in Kettering, Ohio, offers a tip for wax carvers who check the thickness of a wax by holding it up to light. This visual check can be made even easier, Winnie says, by using a lighted bench pin similar to the one he made

> Bubble-foam wrap is an ideal surface for finishing up waxes.

for his own bench. Winnie created a bench pin from setting plastic, which becomes malleable when placed in warm water and hardens at room temperature. He then embedded a nightlight-size fixture and bulb in the plastic and attached it to the back of the pin. He carved out a square opening above the bulb, filled it with a frosted Plexiglas cover plate for light diffusion, and voilá! A source of light at working level. Winnie adds that although the plastic might melt if it overheats, the low-wattage bulb he uses has so far caused him no problems. << By Suzanne Wade >>

CLASSFIED

Subj:

WHY MICHAEL BONDANZA LOVES HIS... CAD PROGRAM

SO TELL US. WHAT'S YOUR SECRET WEAPON?

My CAD program. I currently use Rhino 5.0 for Mac—it's a beta test version that you can't buy yet. They gave it to me to try out. I also use the earlier version of Rhino for PC, which I rely on when I need features that are not implemented in the Mac version yet. They can both run simultaneously on my Mac, using a software program called Boot Camp.

HOW DO YOU USE IT IN YOUR WORK?

It replaces the wax work and some of the metal work I used to do by hand. I can make pretty much any design I want, print it, and have a model. I'll cast it in silver, so I have a fairly close sample of what I want to make, then totally refine it by hand. I don't want a piece to look like it was made by a machine; it's got to look handmade.

WHY DO YOU LOVE IT SO MUCH?

I still use all the same tools at the bench, but CAD makes things go a lot faster. I can make shapes in parts or create patterns that would take hours by hand, but now take minutes. If I wanted to write "I Love You" in fancy letters on a bracelet, I used to build the letters by hand, each one a quarter-inch thick. It was daunting: I'd make them out of silver, push them into wax, pull them out, polish the top of that wax, and cast. Now all I have to do is type out that sentence, and with a few clicks the machine will embed it into the bracelet's surface—it's like using a branding iron. Or I'll make a sweeping pattern, like what my hand engraving looks like, and embed it all over the piece. CAD has also helped me to figure out how to make assembly easier; I can put internal pegs on some parts, especially those that have to be pre-polished and then retrofitted.

WHAT DOES IT ENABLE YOU TO DO THAT NO OTHER TOOL DOES?

It makes me think differently. With model making, you have to think 10 to 15 steps down the road—the better you get, the further down the road you can see. CAD has allowed me to

<21>

see *even further* down the road. But it can also create too many choices, so discipline and a solid sense of what you're seeking are vital. The single most important skill I have is still hand drawing—it's the absolute grounding for everything I do.

WHAT DISCOVERIES OR BREAKTHROUGHS HAVE YOU MADE WITH THIS TOOL?

When I have a design I like, I'll take it another couple of steps and see how much more I can get out of it. For instance, I had a design for a bangle bracelet and wanted to see how it would look as a ring. Previously, that would have been impossible to do unless I wanted to sit and carve wax for hours. But with CAD, I took the bracelet, shrunk it down to the size

of a ring, and printed it. It was spectacular—it was 300 percent smaller and the details were still sharp. And it took about 20 minutes.

REGSTR\\DOC SER#032012

SECRET SHOP TIPS

Preventing Mouse Shoulder

For designers who have switched from pencil and paper to CAD/CAM, the change has brought new aches and pains, especially what Bob Lynn of Lynn's Jewelry in Ventura, California, refers to as "mouse shoulder."

To avoid this stress to the shoulders and neck when spending hours at the computer, Lynn replaced his standard mouse several years ago with a modified trackball. The trackball—a unit featuring a ball that moves freely in its casing—enables designers to modify images much as they would with a mouse. However, because the ball is positioned on the top of unit rather than in its base, a trackball doesn't require a flat surface to operate. This has allowed Lynn to move his base of operations away from his computer table.

He screwed the trackball to a mouse pad using short, dome-head sheet metal screws and a fender washer. "I polished the heads of the screws and the washers to remove any burrs that would cause problems by snagging my pants or whatever it is put on," he notes.

Lynn drilled holes for the screws into the trackball by carefully opening its case and making the holes from the inside out, in areas where there is no circuitry. "The holes should be just big enough to allow the shank of the screw clearance, with the wide sheet-metal threads biting plastic," says Lynn. He then attached beanbag weights to either side of the mouse pad.

Lynn traded in his mouse for a modified trackball.

This mouse pad-trackball combination rested comfortably on his thigh: When Lynn sat down to sketch, he no longer needed to stretch and reach for the mouse. He ultimately replaced the trackball with a wireless 3-D mouse, but he modified that unit as well. Technology advances, but that simple pad, Lynn says, provides "the ultimate ease." **<< By Suzanne Wade >>**

Subj:

WHY ANN CAHOON LOVES HER...
DELRIN DRAWPLATES

SO TELL US. WHAT'S YOUR SECRET WEAPON?

My Delrin drawplates.

HOW DO YOU USE THEM IN YOUR WORK?

I produce a great deal of handmade chain, and every chain I make is finished in these dies. They allow me to reduce the chain's diameter to the proper size, while also achieving a consistent shape and better flexibility.

WHY DO YOU LOVE THEM SO MUCH?

There are a number of things I love.

There are three dies, each with 10 different diameters that generally step up in increments of 0.5 mm (0.25 mm for some of the smaller sizes). In the "small" die, the holes range from 1.5 mm to 5 mm; in the medium, from 3 to 7.5 mm; and in the large, from 8 to 12.5 mm. And each measurement is really what you get! This allows for great consistency and repeatability in a handmade product.

I am also a huge fan of the material from which these dies are made. Delrin is an acetal resin with excellent strength, dimensional stability, and

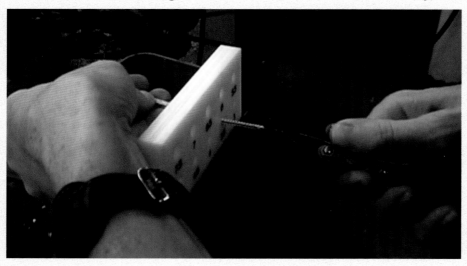

<33>

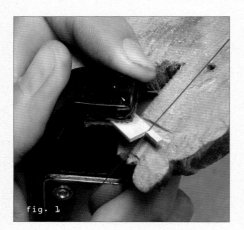

fig. 1

and close along the handle's axis. This can be useful for holding a small piece of bar stock when sawing, for example (Figure 1).

WHAT DISCOVERIES OR BREAKTHROUGHS HAVE YOU MADE WITH THEM?

Discovering the advantages of parallel locking pliers inspired me to mod-ify some of their non-locking cousins. For example, I converted one pair into half-round/flat parallel pliers by grinding one of its jaws; the half-round jaw grips the shank on its inner curve, while the flat jaw grips the outer curve, thus preventing marring (Figure 2). They also greatly reduce the chance that my workpiece will slip out of the jaws, potentially damaging the piece or injuring myself. I like having that kind of security. Why take chances when you don't have to?

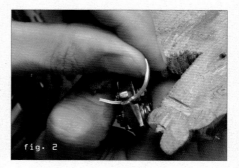

fig. 2

<35>

REGSTR\\DOC SER#032012

SECRET SHOP TIPS

Get a Grip

Working in the shop, you sometimes need to get creative with your tools to "git-r done." Take, for example, the following modifications to a simple pair of pliers, which can be quickly and easily done with a bench grinder or a flex-shaft with a separating disc.

Baby Channel Lock. Available in many hardware stores, the 4.5 inch channel lock has the built in advantage of an adjustable jaw gap. The channel mechanism in these pliers allows for a successively wider gap in four stages, with a maximum of about 25 mm. You can use these pliers to move prongs around a gemstone on many crown assemblies—even very tall ones. To get a better grip on the prongs for such applications, you can modify the jaws in two ways. You can cut a slot down the middle of the lower jaw to better accommodate the prong base on a gallery-type crown. You can also grind the top jaw into a bird-beak form with a slightly concave face to securely hold the top of the prong being moved.

Round-nose Crown Pliers. Take an ordinary pair of round-nose pliers, cut one side so it's 5 to 6 mm shorter than the other side, and give that shorter side an angled, concave face. Heat the tall side, bend it 90 degrees toward the cut side, and grind the face to a slight angle. Configured in this manner, the pliers will hold almost any crown very securely when preparing it for stone setting.

Flat V-prong Closers. A pair of flat pliers can become a safer (and most likely faster) way to close V-prongs (or V-caps) when you evenly grind down the ends of the pliers to an approximate 90 degree angle. It is not so much the closing action of the pliers that moves the V-prong, but rather a rocking and wiggling action applied to the pliers when they are pushed up against the prong.

<< By Gary Dawson and Larry Schultz >>

Editors' Note: If you do any large-scale forging or hot work, you can make a great set of adjustable tongs out of channel-lock pliers, which are durable, reasonably priced, and widely adjustable. Use a surface grinder to remove the teeth and create parallel smooth jaws, which won't badly mar the metal. If you want to go a step further, just TIG weld a set of heavy copper jaws onto them.

CLASSIFIED

Subj:

WHY KATHLEEN DIRESTA LOVES HER...
3M RADIAL FINISHING DISCS

SO TELL US. WHAT'S YOUR SECRET WEAPON?

The 3M Radial Bristle Discs.

WHAT DO THEY DO?

They are fine, spidery, flat brushes [containing grains of aluminum oxide]; you stack them on a mini screw mandrel to sand and polish during the finishing process. They come in a variety of grits/microns, each represented by a different color—green is 50 grit, yellow is 80 grit, etc.

WHY DO YOU LOVE THEM SO MUCH?

These were a wonderful discovery a few years after I started my business, because I do a lot of finishing with sandpaper, either as a stick or as a roll on my flex-shaft. The discs allow me to get into hard-to-reach areas on more sculptural or textured pieces—areas that rigid tools won't allow. Plus the smooth, clean finish allows me to skip the steps of using a satin buff and brass brush with soapy water.

HOW DO YOU USE THEM IN YOUR WORK?

Something I noticed is that they seem to be finer than noted in the catalogs. For example, the yellow is listed at 80 grit, but it's more like a 400 grit sandpaper. So after I file and sand a piece with 220 grit sandpaper, I use yellow discs at the 400 grit level. I then move to red discs, which seem like a 600 grit to me; they smooth the surface and leave a uniform, satin finish. For customers who prefer more shine, I continue with the royal blue, then peach—which gives a shine like a light blue Adalox wheel—then mint green. I'm able to achieve a nice luster, without the mess of polishing compounds.

WHAT DISCOVERIES OR BREAKTHROUGHS HAVE YOU MADE WITH THESE TOOLS?

I realized you can combine colors for different results. If I need to smooth some fine scratches while getting a nice satin finish, I add one red wheel to two yellow wheels. If I use two reds and one blue, I get a finer smooth finish, with a slight sheen.

<37>

Subj:

WHY JASON DOW LOVES HIS... LASER WELDER

SO TELL US. WHAT'S YOUR SECRET WEAPON?

The laser welder.

WHAT DOES IT DO?

It concentrates an adjustable laser beam, heating metal to its melting temperature in a very specific location. Basically you are able to spot-weld without heating an entire piece of metal.

WHY DO YOU LOVE IT SO MUCH?

It's very fun to use. I usually get pretty excited to fire up the laser and get to welding.

HOW DO YOU USE IT IN YOUR WORK?

I use it mostly for a few major purposes. It's great for cleaning up porosity or incomplete fills in castings. I'm also able to tack various pieces into position in preparation for soldering; as I go along I can adjust and readjust components on the fly, making sure everything joins at the right angle or position—almost like sketching in metal. And the laser is the king when it comes to repairs. I can easily replace beads and seats in thin or fragile areas, and it's especially good around heat-sensitive stones.

WHAT DOES IT ENABLE YOU TO DO THAT NO OTHER TOOL DOES?

This tool enables me to work so much faster, which gives me a huge cost advantage. Nonetheless, the biggest plus for me as a designer is that it allows me to join metal like never before and open a whole new world of fabrication. Also, I can keep metal parts springy or work hardened where it may have been impossible to do so otherwise.

WHAT DISCOVERIES OR BREAKTHROUGHS HAVE YOU MADE WITH THIS TOOL?

Ideas and concepts are constantly being invented because of the laser's possibilities. For example, it now becomes possible to encase a pearl entirely in a cage of metal without damaging the pearl. Actually, the biggest things I've discovered lately are a bunch of tricks to get things done less

<39>

painfully. Yes, working with a laser can be physically painful: The metal gets hot as you're holding it, plus the beam can ricochet and zap you in the finger. I now use a wet paper towel to protect my fingers. If I'm doing a bunch of high-heat and re-petitive welding, I'll actually wear a pair of thin and damp white cotton gloves, the kind you use when han-dling jewelry for setting up photog-raphy. One word of caution though: Keep the paper or gloves pretty damp, or you risk them catching on fire...which I can't imagine would be very much fun.

<41>

REGSTR\\DOC SER#032012

SECRET SHOP TIPS

Silver Shield

The pulse from a laser can be focused with pinpoint accuracy—but that doesn't mean it won't sometimes ricochet off the metal. And that reflected energy could cause damage, especially if heat-sensitive stones are positioned nearby. The solution: Use a piece of sterling silver sheet to mask the areas that you want protected. Since silver is highly reflective, it should protect stones and sensitive areas against stray pulses. Just be sure to keep the silver free of the black sooty oxides that can develop: Even though it's reflective, silver will absorb the full impact of the pulse when darkened by oxides or masked with an ink marker. "Plasti-tack" and watchmaker's putty can also be used to protect against ricochets.

<< By Bob Staley >>

Editor's Note: *Another option is to take a pin vise, insert a piece of silver wire in the end, and custom-forge the wire to the desired size necessary to shield the area.*

Sure Shots

If you're having difficulty achieving a solid weld, don't immediately change your laser parameters; instead, try changing the angle at which you're shooting. For example, shoot at the top half or side edge of a prong instead of straight-on with a full beam in a perpendicular fashion. Laser pulses are

Mask sensitive areas with a piece of sterling.

light pulses, and the degree to which they are absorbed or deflected will depend on the nature of the surface and the angle of the shot. If you are shooting at an area that is too absorbent or too reflective, try adjusting the angles to "finesse" the piece and achieve your welding goal. **<< By Bob Staley >>**

CLASSIFIED

Subj:

WHY CHRISTOPHER DUQUET LOVES HIS... ROLLERBALL PEN

SO TELL US. WHAT'S YOUR SECRET WEAPON?

The Uni-Ball Vision Elite Rollerball Pen.

HOW DO YOU USE IT IN YOUR WORK?

To take the purely imaginary into the first step of reality. Drawing will always be the foundation of my work, and the key to creating my own expression of jewelry design.

WHAT DISCOVERIES OR BREAKTHROUGHS HAVE YOU MADE WITH THIS TOOL?

Like many in our industry, I have embraced new technology and use CAD/CAM in my custom jewelry business. But drawing will always be essential to the process. If we depend on machines or others for creativity, our industry will slowly decline until we become irrelevant.

The creative process holds the most pleasure in my endeavors. The design that starts with a sketch on a piece of paper is what separates and distinguishes my work from the multitude of choices available in the field.

<43>

drawing will always be
the foundation
of my work.

CLASSIFIED

Subj:

WHY CYNTHIA EID LOVES HER... MICROFOLD BRAKE

SO TELL US. WHAT'S YOUR SECRET WEAPON?

A microfold brake.

WHAT DOES IT DO?

It allows me to corrugate metal.

WHY DO YOU LOVE IT SO MUCH?

With the strength created by micro-folding and corrugation, I can make large, bold jewelry that is nevertheless very light. I can invent new textures and patterns while adding strength to metal.

HOW DO YOU USE IT IN YOUR WORK?

I begin by corrugating metal sheet. Then I form it gently with hammers or a hydraulic press. The ability to use thin metal not only makes the pieces wearable, but also more affordable from a materials standpoint, which is especially helpful in a time of high metals prices.

WHAT DISCOVERIES OR BREAKTHROUGHS HAVE YOU MADE WITH THIS TOOL?

It enables me to experiment with ideas, materials, and tools, a process that I really enjoy. I can explore the springiness of corrugated metal, or try new combinations of texture and form. My best work is usually designed in this manner, rather than by carefully drawing and planning—which has made me realize that, while I adore my microfold brake, my body is really my most important tool. With my brain, I can figure out how to manipulate metal. Sometimes, it does not matter how fancy the tools that are available—problem-solving is done with that stuff between your ears.

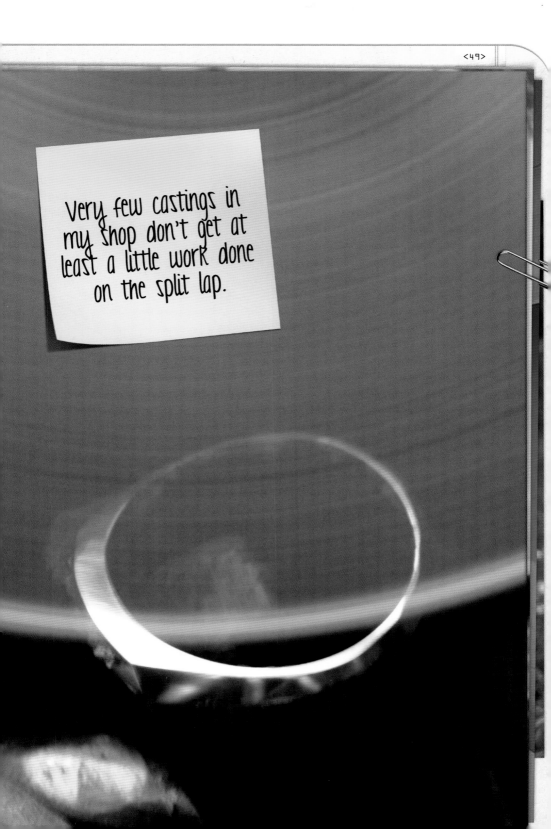

<49>

Very few castings in my shop don't get at least a little work done on the split lap.

split laps come in a variety of diameters and hardnesses, you can choose different laps to suit specific tasks.

WHAT DISCOVERIES OR BREAKTHROUGHS HAVE YOU MADE WITH THIS TOOL?

I have discovered that any surface that will be lapped needs no preparation finer than 80 grit sandpaper. When working on a casting, I use a Cone Loc drum sander to quickly grind off the remaining casting gate, then go straight to the split lap. This enables me to skip any other steps that would be necessary if I didn't

have this tool in my shop, saving me lots of time and energy.

<51>

REGSTR\\DOC SER#032012

SECRET SHOP TIPS

Lip Service

This tip will not only add a margin of safety to your shop, but also some organization. Melting rouge and other polishing compounds can be messy and dangerous if they have low flash points. To add a margin of safety (and reduce bench clutter to boot), try this trick. Heat the compound on a dou-

ble boiler, which will keep the temperature at a safe level. (A soup can makes a great disposable container, by the way.) As it melts, stir the compound with a wooden chopstick; it absorbs much of the compound, so that it becomes a polishing stick itself.

When the compound fully melts, transfer it to a lip-gloss container. Since it will be too thick to pour, you'll

need to scoop it out of the can (use the flattened end of the chopstick). Once the container is filled, re-label the cap with the name of the compound. This will prevent people from using it on their lips, as well as allowing you to find the right compound quickly. Now attach a nail to the back of the container and mount it on your bench, within easy reach.

You can also place the compound in an empty deodorant container. As it fills, lower the platform. Used as an applicator, the container enables minimal contact with the compound.

<< By Arthur Anton Skuratowicz >>

Tin Type

It's really important to keep your compounds and polishers separate. For bench work, we use Altoids tins. You can fill up one tin with melted compound, and have separate tins for the brushes, felts, buffs, and other polishers that you use with the compound. As long as you clean between steps, the polishers will remain uncontaminated and have a long life.

<< By Chris Ploof & Ann Cahoon >>

> Store your compound in a deodorant container.

Subj:

WHY SARAH GRAHAM LOVES HER... STAY SILV BRAZING FLUX

SO TELL US. WHAT'S YOUR SECRET WEAPON?

Stay Silv Black High Temperature Brazing Flux. I would never have been able to grow our business to any degree without this product.

WHAT DOES IT DO?

The flux allows us to solder to cobalt-chrome, which is the metal that [when blackened] is so integral to our look. Cobalt-chrome oxidizes very quickly—any standard jewelry flux burns up long before we are able to flow our solder. Even with Stay Silv we have a very short window in which to make a connection, but the flux shields the metal long enough that, with practice, we are able to make it work.

WHY DO YOU LOVE IT SO MUCH?

Before I learned about Stay Silv, I was able to join the cobalt-chrome only with cold connections, which is labor intensive, less secure, and very limiting in design. I love this flux because it has removed the restrictions that previously constrained our designs. I believe there are two elements that

are key to our success: working with a unique metal and creating uniquely constructed designs. Before finding this flux, the former prevented us from achieving the latter. Now, we are able to pull off both.

HOW DO YOU USE IT IN YOUR WORK?

We prepare our cobalt-chrome for soldering by getting a perfect black finish, and then we remove the oxide in just the areas where we want to solder. We apply the Stay Silv flux to an area and, with a carefully monitored flame, flow our solder. We then reheat the solder and attach whatever it is

<53>

This flux has removed the restrictions that constrained our designs.

we are joining to the cobalt-chrome. We never use the more traditional soldering method of placing two pieces of metal together and pulling the solder through. We need to see the solder flow—it is just too common for the metal to oxidize before the solder has flown for us to be able to trust the more traditional method.

WHAT DOES IT ENABLE YOU TO DO THAT NO OTHER TOOL DOES?

It allows us to make our bread-and-butter item—the diamond stacking ring—beautifully and cost effectively. Stacking rings account for a huge portion of our sales. Without Stay Silv flux we would need to cold join the di-

amonds to the cobalt-chrome shank, which would be cost prohibitive and unattractive! This is true of 95 percent of our entire output; anything that has cobalt-chrome combined with any other metal would be impossible without Stay Silv flux.

WHAT DISCOVERIES OR BREAKTHROUGHS HAVE YOU MADE WITH THIS TOOL?

I learned to not be defeated by cobalt-chrome! Working with this metal is challenging on many levels—casting, soldering, cleaning, cutting, etc. We are constantly striving to overcome, or at least diminish, these challenges, and Stay Silv flux was really a breakthrough. Very few traditional tools in the jewelry catalogs work on this metal, and very few people have worked with it in the way I do, so it can be an overwhelming and lonely road trying to overcome its inherent challenges. But without it, we wouldn't have the business we do—it is our signature. Finding Stay Silv has encouraged me to seek solutions in unlikely places. We have built our business on being unique, and so it only follows that our challenges and solutions will be equally unique!

<55>

REGSTR\\DOC SER#032012

SECRET SHOP TIPS

Sweet Salve

No matter how careful you are in the shop, it's easy to—pardon the pun—get burned. Here are two sweet ways to get quick relief.

Reach for some honey. "The anesthetic effect is amazing, and it has antibiotic properties as well," says Sam Kaffine of *Sterlingbliss.com*. The honey runs as it warms up on your skin, so be sure to secure it with tissue or tape. Kaffine, a former wildland firefighter with the U.S. Forest Service, claims the honey works so well that she's even applied it to firefighters' hands burned so badly that they were too painful to use; after 10 minutes with the honey salve, the firefighters were able to return to work as if nothing had happened.

"I've applied honey to my own steam-burned fingers, swollen with red shiny blisters, and they went back to normal in 15 minutes," Kaffine attests. She keeps single-serving packets of honey in her workshop at all times, right next to the electrical tape she uses to cover cuts.

Vanilla will keep a burn from blistering.

Go for the vanilla. In a post on the Orchid e-mail forum (*ganoksin.com*), jeweler LaVerne Barbare of Gainesville, Florida, suggested this home remedy: "When you burn yourself at the bench (hopefully not too often), use pure vanilla extract on it," she writes. "Soak a cotton ball with the vanilla and tape it to the burn. You will be absolutely amazed how a burn that normally will blister will not with this treatment. A couple of hours later, it's like it never happened. [It's] much better than aloe."

<< By Tina Wojtkielo Snyder >>

CLASSIFIED

Subj:

WHY ALISHAN HALEBIAN LOVES HIS... GRAVER

SO TELL US. WHAT'S YOUR SECRET WEAPON?

If I were stranded on an island somewhere, my espresso machine would be ideal for making my early morning cappuccino and enjoying the beautiful island sunrise. On the other hand, if I had to work also, the tool that is most versatile and helpful is a simple, sharp tool: my graver.

HOW DO YOU USE IT IN YOUR WORK?

Naturally, in the workshop we use the graver to set stones and engrave. However, the graver also comes in very handy when I carve a new model out of wax, or cut, texture, mill, sculpt, etc.

WHY DO YOU LOVE IT SO MUCH?

I love it because it is a simple and versatile tool, and can do a lot more than any other tool. It's handy and there on my bench all the time. The tip could be reshaped and altered for different applications. When I am milling a wax tube, I'll use it to shape and cut the wax while it is spinning,

or open channels. When carving or sculpting, I often use the backside of the graver to texture and burnish the wax. And after a long day of work you can even peel your apple with it. It's useful with any material that is softer than steel.

WHAT DISCOVERIES OR BREAKTHROUGHS HAVE YOU MADE WITH THIS TOOL?

I make my design sketches with a pencil, and I apply the same technique with the graver on metals to achieve complex textures. This method has

<57>

enabled me to achieve certain subtleties in my designs. I apply multiple textures to a piece, one on top of another—a plain texture, then a pattern on top of that, then another plain texture on top of the pattern. It creates a depth and subtlety—you don't see the pattern except at a certain angle.

A few years ago, I went to a Chinese bronze exhibition that had these huge, 3,000-year-old sand-cast vessels, all beautifully done with complex ornamentation. Their makers had none of our technology, but those vessels were almost perfection. For centuries, some of the most beauti-ful jewelry has been made with basic tools—like a graver, which is simply a rod of steel. It's not the tool, it's the person behind the tool that makes the difference.

<59>

REGSTR\\DOC SER#032012

SECRET SHOP TIPS

The Comfort Files

Getting a good grip on your bench tools might require a little creative modification, but it can be well worth the effort—especially if you suffer from carpal tunnel, arthritis, or a number of other hand-related ailments that can strike hard-working bench jewelers.

To make ergonomic handles (which can actually help to prevent some of the aforementioned conditions), you can use JettSett thermoplastic/ceramic fixturing compound. Just mold the compound around your files, pliers, and other hand tools until it conforms to your grip. It will harden into a custom handle.

If you want to make your flex-shaft easier to hold, grab some pre-made pipe insulation and cover it up, advises jeweler Jo Haemer of Timothy W. Green in Portland, Oregon. The soft foam tube isn't slippery and offers a good grip on the flex-shaft and other bench tools.

If you don't want to cover your tool handles, Haemer recommends checking out a product called Gorilla Snot, which musicians use to get a steady grip on guitar picks, drumsticks, bows, and other instruments. You apply the non-gooey refined tree resin to your fingers and it dries in a few seconds, forming a soft, tacky surface that is moisture resistant.

Jeweler Fabio Penuela of Continental Diamond in Minneapolis offers another option for file modification that offers both ergonomic comfort and bench organization. "Sometimes finding the right file for a job can be like finding a needle in a haystack," says Penuela. "To increase efficiency at my bench, I've made my files easy to identify by wrapping colored electrical cable around the handles. I heat-shrunk the electrical cable in place, using different colors to distinguish between smooth and coarse files. In addition to color-coding the files for easier identification, these handles also cushion my hands. They are more comfortable to work with and easier to control."

<< By Tina Wojtkielo Snyder >>

GLASSIFIED

Subj:

WHY BARBARA HEINRICH LOVES HER...
BURNISHER

SO TELL US. WHAT'S YOUR SECRET WEAPON?

My secret weapon is a burnisher.

HOW DO YOU USE IT IN YOUR WORK?

It is used as part of our finishing process. We use the burnisher last, after everything else is done on a piece, to highlight the edges and the details of a design. I also use it like a pencil to draw lines and patterns on the metal, or I run it flat over surfaces to highlight the texture.

WHAT DOES IT ENABLE YOU TO DO THAT NO OTHER TOOL DOES?

The burnisher allows us to define the outline of the piece in a way no other tool can. It especially creates a nice contrast to the matte surfaces we put on our 18k yellow gold pieces. Creating definition between the matte surfaces better brings out the details of a design, and allows the subtleties to find balance.

WHAT DISCOVERIES OR BREAKTHROUGHS HAVE YOU MADE WITH THIS TOOL?

We use the burnisher on 99 percent of our pieces, and it has allowed us to establish a very distinctive gold look. I can highlight the veins in a roller-printed leaf or petal, for instance, or burnish the raised areas in hammered pieces. It is a look that cannot be achieved by mass finishing techniques, such as tumbling, or by other hand finishes, such as wheel polishing.

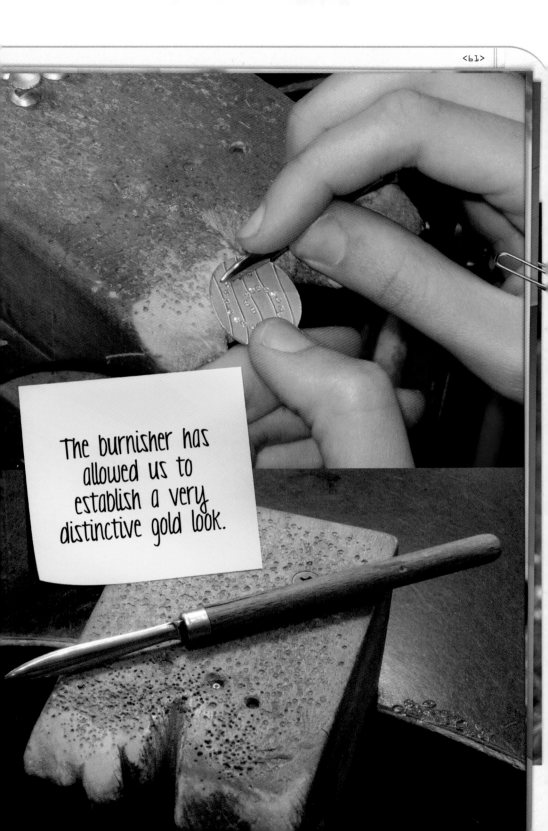

<61>

The burnisher has allowed us to establish a very distinctive gold look.

CLASSIFIED

Subj:

WHY CHARLIE HERNER LOVES HIS...
SUPER CERAMIC STONE FLAT POLISHING SET

SO TELL US. WHAT'S YOUR SECRET WEAPON?

The Super Ceramic Stone Flat Polishing Set.

WHAT DOES IT DO?

It allows me to clean up and polish extremely detailed areas that I otherwise couldn't effectively access.

HOW DO YOU USE IT IN YOUR WORK?

I use the strips in areas that I can't reach with a file or with sandpaper. In the past, to polish these hard-to-reach areas I would rely on a pin tumbler or "thrumming" [i.e., using a string or cord charged with compound]. Now, with grits from 120 to 1,200, the stone sticks allow me to take a piece all the way from a raw casting to a pre-polished stage.

WHAT DOES IT ENABLE YOU TO DO THAT NO OTHER TOOL DOES?

I'm able to shape the stone's surface, which allows me to keep the details of the piece crisp and well preserved. These sticks are great for cleaning up pieces with tight spaces and recessed flat areas, such as Celtic knots and trellis work. Pin tumbling and thrumming are more of a random, overall approach that can leave surface defects and also lead to loss of detail. But the sticks can be precisely applied and create a drastically cleaner finished surface. Working in an environment with several jewelers, I find that these sticks are always being  borrowed multiple times each week.

WHAT DISCOVERIES OR BREAKTHROUGHS HAVE YOU MADE WITH THIS TOOL?

I have found that you can apply a brush-like finish to recessed flat areas, whereas most jewelers would apply a sandblasted finish due to lack of access. You can also, depending on the grit used, apply matte finishes to detailed areas. Quality work lies in the details, and this tool allows me to refine each piece that I work on.

These sticks are great for cleaning up pieces with tight spaces.

CLASSIFIED

Subj:

WHY LISA KRIKAWA LOVES HER... HYDRAULIC PRESS DIE

SO TELL US. WHAT'S YOUR SECRET WEAPON?

Hydraulic die press.

HOW DO YOU USE IT IN YOUR WORK?

I use it to create simple to complex three-dimensional designs from sheet metal—predominantly pendants, earrings, and lockets.

WHY DO YOU LOVE IT SO MUCH?

It's just so mechanical—a simple but powerful tool. It's basically a plate that enables you to force sheet metal into a die cavity to create a three-dimensional form. You can also achieve different textures, pressing precious metal into forms for heavy mesh or perforated metal. I love how the

metal responds like fabric, sliding effortlessly into place. There's nothing fancy about it—except the complex textures and shapes that it allows you to achieve for jewelry.

WHAT DOES IT ENABLE YOU TO DO THAT NO OTHER TOOL DOES?

With this tool, you can give a piece of sheet metal so much body and still retain its light weight, since you are using a very thin piece of metal (I prefer 24 gauge). Many of the designs I make with the press could

<65>

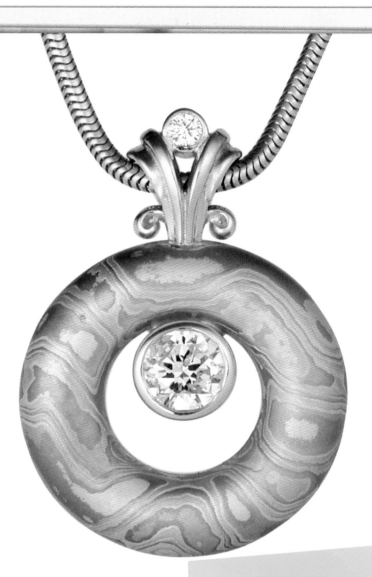

You can give metal
so much body and
still retain its
light weight.

never be made solid because they would be too heavy—and much too expensive. As long as the design's outline is symmetrical, you can press two pieces into the same die and then solder them together, and they will fit perfectly.

WHAT DISCOVERIES OR BREAKTHROUGHS HAVE YOU MADE WITH THIS TOOL?

I've learned a lot about making dies using the hydraulic press. To create the female die into which the metal is pressed, I usually either carve it out of aluminum or make it out of liquid steel. Although neoprene is frequently used as the male die, plastic and metal can also work well, particularly for deep or detailed forms: They help the metal move down into the cavity, preserving the thickness of the sheet. (Conversely, when you use neoprene for the male die, you actually pinch the metal to the flat die face and force the remaining metal to be stretched into the die, making it much thinner.) By using very thin sheet metal, you can achieve even more complex patterns. I can get such a detailed piece out of a carved aluminum block using 26 gauge metal—there are so many curves and ins and outs that the design of the piece becomes very strong. It's hard to believe that it started out as a piece of sheet metal.

<6b7>

REGSTR\\DOC SER#032012

SECRET SHOP TIPS

Fine Grind

If you use an ultrasonic cleaner to clean jewelry after it's been on the polishing wheel, the black residue at the bottom of your ultrasonic tank is full of precious metal. You can recover this metal simply by using a paper coffee filter, says Jim Stewart of Stewart's International Jewelry School in Jupiter, Florida. Place the coffee filter inside a strainer and balance the strainer on a large can or bowl. Pour the solution through the filter to strain it. The filter will capture any precious particles floating in the solution.

Next, use a paper towel to wipe the sludge out of the tank. Put the coffee filter and paper towel inside a plastic trash bag reserved specifically for precious-metal waste. (Try to keep metals segregated as best as possible.) When the bag is full, send it to a refinery. You can pour the used solution back into the ultrasonic tank, adding a little non-ammoniated concentrate to freshen it.

<< By Suzanne Wade >>

Foiled Again

How can you tell when the ultrasonic stops working? If it refuses to turn on or does something dramatic, like catch fire, you probably don't have many doubts about its usefulness. If you're not sure, though, try this field test, which was passed on by Mike Fritz of Lone Star Technical Services in San Antonio, which specializes in the repair of ultrasonic cleaners. Cut a piece of aluminum foil 1 inch shorter than the long axis of your tank. Turn on the machine and immerse the foil vertically into the tank until it is about a half inch from the bottom. (Be sure not to let it touch the ends or sides of the tank.) Run the machine for 30 seconds and remove the foil.

"You should see a pattern of dents and/or holes evenly distributed on the foil," Fritz says. "If the pattern is asymmetrical or non-existent, you have an indication that the machine is not functioning properly and should be sent for repair. We use this test daily, and it has proven an effective indicator of a unit's function."

<< By Suzanne Wade >>

Subj:

WHY LEE KROMBHOLZ LOVES HIS...
GRS GRAVERMAX

SO TELL US. WHAT'S YOUR SECRET WEAPON?

The GRS GraverMax with two hand-pieces: a hammer handpiece and an engraving handpiece.

WHAT DOES IT DO?

It is an air-powered, foot-controlled tool to assist with hammering and engraving, with very flexible applications. It increases the precision and speed of almost every style of stone setting and engraving. Without it, I would have to retire. I actually have two GraverMaxes, just in case one breaks down (which seldom happens).

WHY DO YOU LOVE IT SO MUCH?

It takes my setting and engraving work to a whole other level. Bezel setting emeralds—no problem! Hand engraving a custom wedding ring—it is fun! The GraverMax also increases my work speed and accuracy, making my time more valuable. With it, I am "Super Jeweler!"

WHAT DOES IT ENABLE YOU TO DO THAT NO OTHER TOOL DOES?

I can offer my customers a higher level of service that jewelers without my secret weapon can't. I can provide hand engraving in my designs, for example, without needing a specialist on staff or needing to outsource this work. I have always loved to carve shanks on engagement and wedding rings, but fatigue was an issue. Figure 1 [page 70] shows an example of an engagement ring that I completely carved and engraved with the assistance of my GraverMax. While much

<69>

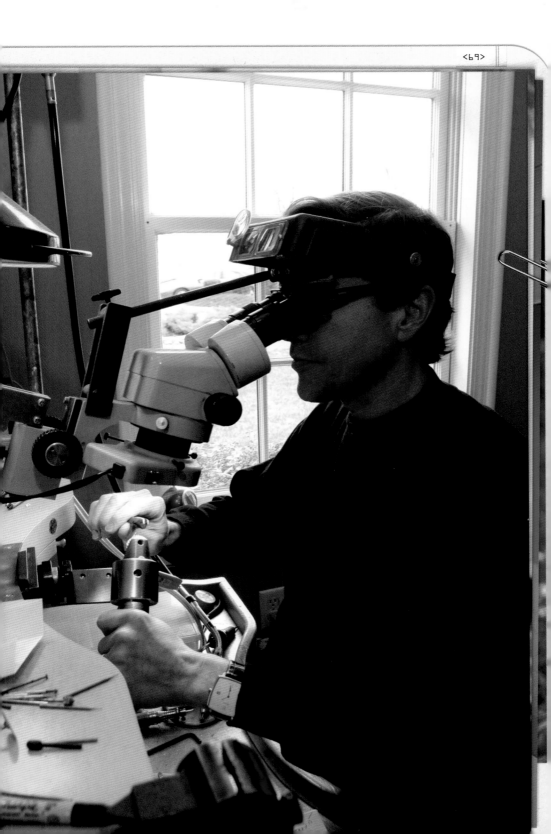

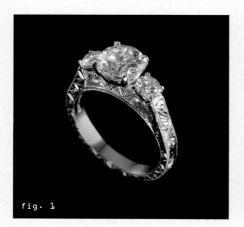

fig. 1

fig. 2

of this detail can be achieved by hand, the level of fatigue that occurs when hand-pushing a graver in harder metals makes for a long struggle. Since purchasing the GraverMax, I can engrave and carve all day long and get the flowing lines I am looking for.

WHAT DISCOVERIES OR BREAKTHROUGHS HAVE YOU MADE WITH THIS TOOL?

I have been able to tackle difficult jobs and make quantum leaps in the quality that I am able to produce. My jewelry work is something I can be proud

of even under a microscope (which I use in tandem with the GraverMax). For example, I made one ring [Figure 2] in which the entire mounting was covered by pavé-set tsavorite garnets; that would have been very hard to do without the GraverMax. No other tool puts this level of power and control at my fingertips. I have tried adding reciprocating hammer attachments to my flex-shaft, but the combination of the vibration and singular level of power made for limited use. The GraverMax has sat next to my bench for 20 years and is used every day.

<71>

REGSTR\\DOC SER#032012

SECRET SHOP TIPS

Setting Pretty

A special challenge for jewelers doing production pavé or channel setting is seating the diamonds evenly and keeping them in place while completing the setting process. To make the task easier, David Winnie of F&J Manufacturing in Kettering, Ohio, suggests using soft wax, a dental spatula, and a bit of old nylon pantyhose.

Your new setting tools: a dental spatula and nylon pantyhose.

First, place all the stones into the channel or pavé area, Winnie says. Then apply a film of soft wax and press it in around the stones with your fingers or with a very small dental spatula. The wax Winnie uses is a soft, low-temperature, pliable wax sold as "sculpture wax" in most catalogs.

Wipe off the excess wax with an old diamond cloth, which has less lint than many other cloths; you'll need to press hard to clear away the unnecessary wax. Inspect the piece to make sure that all the stones are seated properly.

Work the channel or beads about half-down or half-tight (just enough so the diamonds are stitched in), then steam out the wax. The best way to do this is to wrap the piece tightly in a fine mesh nylon filter screen, such as old pantyhose, and steam.

"Any stones that don't stay put will at least stay close," Winnie notes. You can then tighten the settings as usual. "Since we use a Gravermax, all the loose stones give a good visual by jiggling merrily until they are tightened." << **By Suzanne Wade** >>

Subj:

WHY BLAINE LEWIS LOVES HIS... NSK MICROMOTOR

SO TELL US. WHAT'S YOUR SECRET WEAPON?

The NSK micromotor with the reduction gear. It's the absolute Porsche of bearing cutting.

HOW DO YOU USE IT IN YOUR WORK?

I use it for all forms of diamond and stone setting: cutting small parts, grinding, polishing—most anything for which I would have previously used a flex-shaft. I use my micromotor almost exclusively now.

WHY DO YOU LOVE IT SO MUCH?

The NSK has a 4:1 reduction gear that takes 30,000 rpm down to 9,500, all torque. That's more than enough for jewelry; I rarely go above 4,000 rpm. And it runs vibration free, without shudder. A bur wobble can wreck a piece, and when you screw up a bearing in platinum or gold, that can be an expensive "oopsie." The NSK is also very compact—there isn't a motor hanging up in the air, no cord to bind or twist. It's the ultimate freedom.

WHAT DOES IT ENABLE YOU TO DO THAT NO OTHER TOOL DOES?

I can work longer because of lack of fatigue. I used to have to get up and down to adjust my flex-shaft height, all day long. Now I don't have to do that; I'm not tethered to a hanging motor. It eases my workday and allows me to do not only more work, but better work.

It's the absolute Porsche of bearing cutting.

<73>

Subj:

WHY EVA MARTIN LOVES HER... THINKPAD

SO TELL US. WHAT'S YOUR SECRET WEAPON?

I couldn't do the job I do without my ThinkPad.

WHAT DOES IT DO?

So much. It's how I create and update my website—which is how I get my customers. It's the tool I use to communicate my designs to my clients. It's how I research ideas and how I find the impossible-to-find stone. It runs the Rhino CAD software I use to create many of my pieces. I would be lost without it.

WHY DO YOU LOVE IT SO MUCH?

I love it because it's the perfect complement to time-honored skills of fine goldsmithing. I trained to be a jeweler at North Bennet Street School in Boston. Their program teaches fine craftsmanship and technical mastery through intensive hands-on training. It's wonderful to be able to supplement those skills with the advances in new technology; it opens up a world of new possibilities.

HOW DO YOU USE IT IN YOUR WORK?

Almost all of my work is made on commission, and I rarely meet the people who commission me; almost all communication with them is done over e-mail on my ThinkPad. Once they've told me their story, the first thing I do is research through my laptop—a good design rarely comes from thin air, it's born from research. I then create photorealistic renderings using CAD for my clients to view, wherever they happen to be. More often than not, I create the piece using CAD and upload it to be printed in wax and then cast.

<79>

Gravers are some of the most under-appreciated tools on the bench.

soon as you're done texturing, you're finished.)

In addition, I do a lot of wax carving with gravers. If you can create it in wax with a graver, you can finish it in metal. This is particularly relevant today, considering all of the CAD/CAM pieces that are modeled and cast, then can't be properly finished in metal because you can't get into the little nooks and crannies you created in CAD. Doing wax work with a graver will ensure that, by using that same graver, you'll be able to get into any recess on the casting.

WHAT DISCOVERIES OR BREAKTHROUGHS HAVE YOU MADE WITH THIS TOOL?

I made a lathe using my flex-shaft handpiece (Figure 3); it allows me to rotate a small cylinder of wax in a stationary setup, so I can use my gravers to shape it into bands and bezels. I've also made a lot of my own gravers and modified commercial gravers to suit my needs. Customizing the profile of a graver allows you to create unique textures and patterns, and to differentiate your jewelry from the mass-market pack. The options are truly endless.

fig. 3

<81>

SECRET SHOP TIPS

Making a Brass Stone-Seating Tool

When setting stones, jewelers value any tool that gives them greater flexibility. One easy way to create your own "seating tool" is to take a 1/8 inch pointed brass rod, mount it in a graver handle, and taper the rod's point to a flat end. By applying a bit of adhesive such as sticky wax to the top, you can use it to hold and seat small stones more easily. But why stop there? For even greater control, use a tiny ball bur to grind out a hemispherical dip in the top. The softer edges of the dip will better cradle the table and crown facets of the stone, allowing for better positioning with less trauma to the facet junction. The dip can also be packed with wax, so you can always have a sticky tip that will release the stone as needed.

<< By Arthur Anton Skuratowicz >>

Heads Up

When soldering heads onto a ring, you need to prepare the hole or opening in the ring to match the base of the head. There are burs specifically designed for this process, but although similar in shape and size to a base, they are not exact matches. For a better fit, grind a bullet-shaped silicone abrasive to match the angle and curvature of the base. This enables you to match each opening more precisely, resulting in improved solder adhesion and more accurate positioning.

You can go one step further by using a lathe or a flex-shaft to modify a metal, wooden, or plastic mandrel. Once the mandrel matches the angle and shape of the base, cut a slit down its center. Insert your abrasive film of choice, wrap it around the mandrel, and secure. You now have a handy tool that can not only create a better fit between the opening in the ring and the base of the head, but also allow you to attach different abrasives as needed, providing greater versatility.

<< By Arthur Anton Skuratowicz >>

CLASSIFIED

Subj:

WHY JOEL MCFADDEN LOVES HIS... MEIJI MICROSCOPE

SO TELL US. WHAT'S YOUR SECRET WEAPON?

The Meiji microscope.

WHY DO YOU LOVE IT SO MUCH?

Now I can really see what I am doing— I couldn't believe the difference in my work. Like most old-school jewelers, I was trained to set by feel. I was always struggling to do better work, but I couldn't see what was going on. Now I set everything with the micro-

scope. My slogan is, If it looks good under the scope, it will look great to the naked eye. In addition, my back and neck have healed. I was suffering from pinched nerves in my neck due to the sitting position I was using at the bench. The Meiji allows me to

keep my head straight and drop my work area, relieving the stress. This tool has both made me a better bench jeweler and prolonged my career.

HOW DO YOU USE IT IN YOUR WORK?

We examine every piece that comes into our shop under the microscope, and I do all of the setting and some of the finishing work under it. We are known for our detailed finish work and micro pavé setting, all of which is done using the microscope. We polish a lot of pieces with micro burnishers and dental floss, and the microscope

<83>

If it looks good
under the scope,
it will look great to
the naked eye.

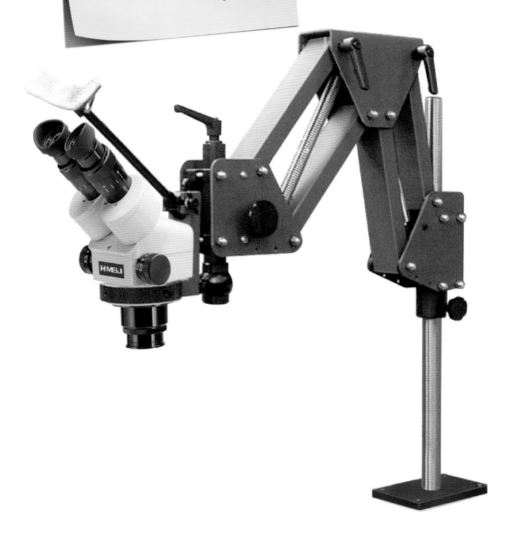

makes it much easier to get in those little nooks and crannies.

WHAT DISCOVERIES OR BREAKTHROUGHS HAVE YOU MADE WITH THIS TOOL?

I was trained to set most stones with a 90 degree bur. However, traditional setting burs tend to cut sloppy seats, which can result in stone damage and loss. Using the microscope, I have learned to set most stones with micro ball burs and inverted cones [to create a more secure fit]. Case in point: I recently got a ring back that I had created, a 2 carat radiant with two trillions. The customer had another jeweler size down the ring, and he did a poor job. When the customer dropped the ring in a grocery store, it snapped in two at one of the seams and at the trillion. The trillion was still in the ring, held by just two prongs, with one point hanging out in mid air—but she didn't lose the stone. That is a testament to proper setting. I don't know of another tool out there that will teach a jeweler to be better at his or her craft than the Meiji.

<85>

SECRET SHOP TIPS

Watchful Eye

Sometimes, a common shop tool can save your reputation. When a customer recently approached Daniel Spirer of Daniel R. Spirer Jewelers in Cambridge, Massachusetts, with a diamond that he had purchased elsewhere, Spirer sketched out options for the customer and the two agreed on a design. Although the diamond had a certificate, Spirer decided to take the prudent course of action and check the diamond under a microscope before beginning any work on the ring—and boy, was he glad that he did.

The certificate stated that the diamond was 1.23 carats, G color, SI2 clarity. While the color and clarity were a match, the plot of the stone did not match the plot on the certificate. On the latter, the plot showed a distinctive grouping of inclusions in the middle of the table, whereas on the diamond, there was only a tiny pinpoint on the table and all of the inclusions were around the sides of the stone. Upon further inspection, Spirer found that the dimensions of the diamond were very slightly different from those indicated on the certificate—but the difference was more than what could be attributed to tool calibration.

"I had a feeling that somewhere down the line someone had two stones that were the same size, color, and clarity, and they accidently switched them," says Spirer. "I don't believe that the seller was aware of the problem, and the customer got the quality of stone that he thought he was getting, but the issue here is that I found the problem just in time."

Had Spirer not carefully inspected the diamond under magnification and proceeded with crafting the ring for the customer, the potential lawsuits down the line could have been catastrophic to his business. "If I hadn't checked it and the customer took it to another jeweler later to confirm it was his stone, I could have been accused of switching stones," says Spirer. "That would be the end of my reputation and could conceivably cost me a small fortune in legal fees."

The moral of the story, according to Spirer, is "If you're going to be serious about dealing with diamonds, you need a microscope."

<< By Tina Wojtkielo Snyder >>

CLASSIFIED

Subj:

WHY MICHELLE PAJAK-REYNOLDS LOVES HER... LINDSTROM RX PLIERS AND CUTTER SET

SO TELL US. WHAT'S YOUR SECRET WEAPON?

The Lindstrom Rx Pliers and Cutter Set: flat-nose, round-nose, chain-nose, and flush cutter.

HOW DO YOU USE THEM IN YOUR WORK?

I use them for wirework, stringing pearls and gemstones, and crimping.

WHY DO YOU LOVE THEM SO MUCH?

They're the perfect set of pliers—I can take them anywhere! The tools have super-comfortable ergonomic grips, as well as an adjustable "BioSpring"—a little spring between the handles that limits the resistance when I squeeze them.

WHAT DO THEY ENABLE YOU TO DO THAT NO OTHER TOOL DOES?

I can work all day without pain! The chain-nose pliers are also great for getting into really tiny spaces that do not allow for regular crimping pliers.

WHAT DISCOVERIES OR BREAKTHROUGHS HAVE YOU MADE WITH THESE TOOLS?

I bought my Lindstrom pliers almost 10 years ago. At the time, I was working on a gallery show featuring pieces that required thousands of crimp beads and lots of tiny wirework. After working in the studio every day for 12 to 16 hours, my hands and arms were throbbing with pain. I bought

the Rx pliers just hoping that the ergonomic handles would make working those long hours more comfortable. I had no idea that after a few days of using them, the pain I was feeling would disappear! After using these pliers for so long, my hand muscles have "memorized" how to make jewelry with them. Anytime I have to use other pliers, what I'm attempting to create just doesn't come out right.

<B7>

CLASSIFIED

Subj:

WHY CHRIS PLOOF LOVES HIS... MINIATURE STAKES

SO TELL US. WHAT'S YOUR SECRET WEAPON?

My miniature forming, raising, and bezel stakes, especially the system developed by Bill Fretz [of Fretz Design in Bucksport, Maine].

HOW DO YOU USE THEM IN YOUR WORK?

They allow me to precisely form and fit bezels to all shapes of stones—I can easily make small hollow forms and rings with them.

WHY DO YOU LOVE THEM SO MUCH?

My first stake was a very small anvil with two horns: one round, the other flat. It was made in France, and I think I paid $3 for it at a flea market. It sat on my bench for a while. Then one day I had made a bezel that was a tiny bit small. I grabbed the stake, along with a miniature goldsmith's hammer, and went to work. I have a background in blacksmithing, and all of a sudden I realized I could easily customize the angles and size of the bezel by using the [hammer's] flat face and the cross peen, along with

the round horn and square edges of the miniature anvil. A few years later I met Bill Fretz at a trade show. I was admiring his tools when he started to tell me what they were used for—shaping bezels. I told him I instinctively knew; I had been using a poor man's version. It was love at first sight. His stakes are beautiful, well made, easy to use, and come in a variety of shapes.

WHAT DO THEY ENABLE YOU TO DO THAT NO OTHER TOOL DOES?

They allow for precision bezels custom made for each situation, and give me the same freedom that hammers

and anvils give to larger projects: I can customize miniature free-form

<89>

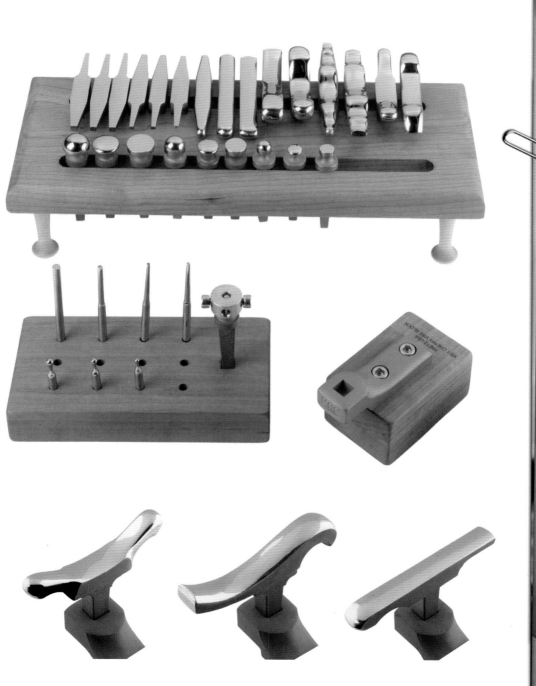

shapes in nearly endless variety. They enable me to create large-volume hollow forms at mid-volume prices!

WHAT DISCOVERIES OR BREAKTHROUGHS HAVE YOU MADE WITH THESE TOOLS?

Well, nothing as important as the cure for tendonitis or vaccinations for common viruses. I just enjoy using them: They bring me back to the basics, away from all of my machines. Two of the most basic elements in our craft are hammers and a hammering surface. Miniature stakes take me back to that, and allow me to have a deep connection with the material and the process.

<91>

REGSTR\\DOC SER#032012

SECRET SHOP TIPS

Popsicle Trick

Steven Lubecki, a jeweler at Chris Ploof Designs Inc. in Pawtucket, Rhode Island, is obsessive about perfect finishes. And to get the best finishes possible on even the most complicated, detailed pieces, Lubecki relies on an unorthodox jewelry tool: Popsicle sticks.

He lines up a row of about 20 Popsicle sticks (which are readily available at craft stores), leaving just a hairline of space between them. He then applies Elmer's glue to the back of a sheet of sandpaper, places the sheet on top of the sticks, and weighs it down. Once the glue dries, he writes the sandpaper grit on each stick, using a colored Sharpie marker. (Each grit has a separate color in his coding system.) Now he can tell at a glance the grit on the stick.

He then cuts out a few sticks with a utility knife and tailors each to suit his needs. Lubecki likes Popsicle sticks because they are somewhat flexible but provide a good, consistent backing for the sandpaper.

"I carve the tips of the sticks down with a utility knife into points or flats, and I sometimes whittle down the back of the stick so it's really thin if I need to get into a thin area," says Lubecki. "Because the surface area is so small, the sticks wear out quickly. Once I wear out one end, I just cut it off and sharpen the stick back up with my knife. It's like sharpening a pencil."

Line up about 20 Popsicle sticks and glue sandpaper sheets to their backs.

The remaining sheet of sandpaper sticks is stored in an accordion-style file folder. Each slot in the folder holds a different grit and keeps the sheets organized, neat, and flat. Lubecki simply dips into the folder as needed, cuts off and shapes a few sticks for the task at hand, and uses them to feed his obsession for the perfect finish.

<< By Tina Wojtkielo Snyder >>

CLASSFIED

Subj:

WHY TODD REED LOVES HIS... LATHE

SO TELL US. WHAT'S YOUR SECRET WEAPON?

I like having a lathe in the studio for many reasons. The machine is basic in concept and super-deep in versatility and value.

WHAT DOES IT DO?

The lathe allows us to make stock, parts, tools, and/or master models very quickly and accurately. It consists of a few major components/elements—mainly a headstock, a tailstock, and a carriage—that work together in a mechanically delicious way. The headstock has a chuck and spindle that holds the part being turned, the carriage supports the sliding tool that will cut the spinning part, and the tailstock has additional tooling.

HOW DO YOU USE IT IN YOUR WORK?

The machine is used daily to carve ring bands from stock, drill holes in eternity bands, turn channels for channel settings, carve tapers out of stock for bezels, make masters in wood or wax... This is a tool that gets

used by all smiths in our shop every day!

WHAT DOES IT ENABLE YOU TO DO THAT NO OTHER TOOL DOES?

It gives me the versatility to do anything in-house with accuracy and ease, and the steps can be consistently repeated for production methods. Eternity bands, for example, can be fabricated and turned with a high degree of precision and quality compared with casting. The machine helps us to save both time and money.

WHY DO YOU LOVE IT SO MUCH?

There's an element I love about being with the metal—actually working the volume of metal, rather than relying on a process that removes the operator completely. There is a certain level of romance and allure that comes with machining metal, and I simply do not know why.

WHAT DISCOVERIES OR BREAKTHROUGHS HAVE YOU MADE WITH THIS TOOL?

In our town there's a local master

<93>

craftsman—a guru of all related to gold, gemstones, and machines—named Lew Wackler, who many years ago took the time to teach me about the insane amount of opportunity the lathe could offer a small workshop. We now have a level of accuracy, cleanliness, and versatility I would never have had otherwise, and [the lathe] has given my work an inherent "machined" look that it otherwise would not have. There is so much opportunity with the machine... I made a teapot and a set of tea cups with Lew in his workshop, and he used the lathe to cut and

carve the gemstone top on the teapot. I would say we use only 5 percent of the machine's capabilities.

REGSTR\\DOC SER#032012

SECRET SHOP TIPS

Industrial Strength

Don't ignore industrial suppliers. They have a nearly endless variety of small parts and tools that you may find useful, and offer metals not stocked by typical jewelry supply houses. For instance, they are a good source of carbide tooling for small mills and lathes, which is especially useful for cutting directly in metal. While carbide tooling is more expensive than high-speed steel tools, it's much longer lasting and can be used with less thought toward flood cooling. (It can be advantageous to not have oil spraying around to keep tools cool, especially in a small shop.) However, keeping tools cool will extend their life, so you could also search industrial suppliers for a positionable airline. When connected to an air compressor, the line directs a flow of cooling—and chip-clearing—air at your workpiece.

<< By Chris Ploof >>

Take a Second Look

It's been said that one man's trash is another man's treasure, and I'll vouch for that. I've done quite well by "scrounging"—looking into other industries and finding new uses for items that other people have cast off as broken, worn out, or obsolete, or are simply too familiar with to see the additional value. For example:

• A set of five chasing tools sold on eBay for $40, while a box of 80 to 100 watchmaker's staking tools sold for just $20. Watchmaker's tools, you see, are considered obsolete and good only for fixing watches. Ah, but those tools are made of the same hardened and tempered steel as the chasing tools, and can be easily altered to suit your needs.

• Need a good soldering pick? Your local bike shop will certainly have titanium spokes on hand, and it'll usually give away the bent ones for free. A free titanium pick, perfect for platinum!

• A 50 mm camera lens can act as a giant, high quality loupe, and you can pick one up for free (or cheaply) from a camera shop if the diaphragm inside is broken. The optics are great on such a lens, and the field of view is large.

If you look at things in the right way, you're bound to see something others don't—including a healthier bottom line. << By Charles Lewton-Brain >>

Subj:

WHY ALAN REVERE LOVES HIS...
DIGITAL SLIDE CALIPER

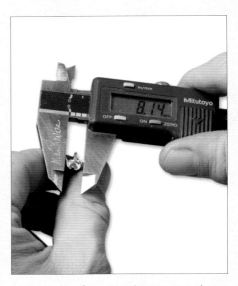

SO TELL US. WHAT'S YOUR SECRET WEAPON?

The digital slide caliper.

WHY DO YOU LOVE IT SO MUCH?

I like to measure things—it's the one way that I understand the world around me—and this tool is very accurate: It measures the world to within 1/100 of a millimeter. It is easy to read and fits in my pocket.

HOW DO YOU USE IT IN YOUR WORK?

I use it all the time to obtain inside and outside diameters, depths, straight edges, and right angles. It can also inscribe lines to lay out measurements, parallel lines, and more. And it serves as a straight edge for both measurement and layout.

WHAT DISCOVERIES OR BREAKTHROUGHS HAVE YOU MADE WITH THIS TOOL?

Although it was not designed for this purpose, the digital slide caliper doubles as precision parallel pliers. For example, prior to setting, you

can use it when moving prongs in or out in preparation for a certain size gemstone. If you calculate the stone's diameter plus the thickness of one prong, you have the ideal outside distance between two opposing prongs. Rather than pushing the prongs in and out individually with a pusher or pliers, you can use the digital slide caliper as a pair of pliers to squeeze the prongs together to the precise measurement. If a prong springs back after release, close it down incrementally, testing to see when it rests in the correct position.

<97>

It measures the world to within 1/100 of a millimeter.

Subj:

WHY CORRIE SILVIA LOVES HER...
CHASING AND REPOUSSÉ TOOLS

SO TELL US. WHAT'S YOUR SECRET WEAPON?

My chasing and repoussé tools! Some tools I have purchased (and later modified), but many I have made myself from tool-steel stock.

WHAT DO THEY DO?

They move and shape sheet metal. I use my liner tools (dull, flat, chisel-like punches) to transfer my initial design to the metal, and then again in the final stages to add detail—either organic or geometric shapes that are slightly sharp and give the metal depth. I use my ball punches and daps to stretch the metal quickly to form an overall shape, and my planishing tools to smooth the metal to a hard, even, shiny surface.

HOW DO YOU USE THEM IN YOUR WORK?

Together, these tools enable me to give the metal volume, form, and texture. Typically I work in copper, and the softness of the metal responds easily to the tools. I'll make design decisions based on the way the piece feels and how it moves with the blows of the hammer and punch. If I'm trying to represent a hurricane, for example, I'll choose the basic direction of the moving winds, but use the inherent qualities of the copper to help form the piece, so the lines appear natural and flowing. I work each section of the metal, hammering and chasing across the surface, adding stipples, cross hatches, planished surfaces, and curves, until the peaks are sharp and the textures flow.

<99>

WHY DO YOU LOVE THEM SO MUCH?

This sounds a bit artsy, but I get lost in the monotonous constancy of the hammer, hearing the constant *tap, tap, tap* as I texture away the imperfections and give the metal life and vibrancy. The physical effort of moving and texturing the metal becomes addictive, and as the soft, curved lines and stippled textures begin to flow, they become sensual and almost painterly. I find the whole process to be wonderfully calming.

WHAT DO THEY ENABLE YOU TO DO THAT NO OTHER TOOL DOES?

Engraving, etching, stamping, roll printing, etc., are all wonderful techniques to texture metal, and I have used all of them. But none alone give me the variety and clarity of texture that chasing and repoussé tools provide. These tools let me articulate patterns on the surface that range from busy and ornate to calm and soft—I can replicate nature with thousands of marks, or just one. Often I use differently shaped tools to layer hammer marks over one another, adding depth and helping to guide the viewer's eye. I also use the tools to stretch the metal to its thinnest limits, so that it has a volume exceeding its typical boundaries. Etching and engravings would not be able to provide such variation and depth.

WHAT DISCOVERIES OR BREAKTHROUGHS HAVE YOU MADE WITH THIS TOOL?

Chasing and repoussé are among the oldest techniques in metalworking and jewelry history, so I think there is little I have discovered that would add to the greater good of the industry. However, I have learned a great deal about how to best manipulate metal and guide its movement into

forms. I have learned that controlling metal and forcing it to work in one direction can be counterintuitive, and that you have to follow the basic laws of the metal in which you are working. I've also gained an understanding of how to juxtapose metal's malleability with its rigidity, and to use layer upon layer of texture, something that I feel distinguishes my work. I love chasing and repoussé; with only hardened tool steel separating me from the metal, I can feel connected to my art in a way that other processes don't allow.

<101>

REGSTR\\DOC SER#032012

SECRET SHOP TIPS

In Good Form

Looking for a suitable surface on which to hammer the hours away? After spending a small fortune on dapping and forming tools, one jeweler who belongs to the Orchid e-mail forum (*ganoksin.com*) put out a call: What are the best surfaces on which to form silver into 3-D objects? He got many suggestions, a handful of which follow:

What are the best surfaces to dap and form silver?

• As an alternative to lead blocks—a popular metal-forming platform before health hazards were brought to the forefront—Hratch Babikian of Philadelphia suggests using a lead-free pewter bench block for chasing and repoussé, which he says works just as well as lead and is non-toxic. "It comes in ingot form [so] that you can cast it in any shape to suit your needs," he writes.

• Sandbags are also great, adds Babikian. "If you are working large enough, as in feet and not inches, you can use straight sand in a large container." For smaller jewelry-size objects, he suggests Delrin blocks.

• For chasing and repoussé work, James Miller of London and Surrey, England, keeps a selection of close-grain hardwood blocks with various shaped hollows in their surfaces and edges. "I cut and shape them to suit each job," he says.

• Lastly, red pitch is the jeweler's old standby for repoussé. To avoid a mess, Victoria Lansford of Atlanta suggests spraying a piece with Pam cooking spray before putting it into the pitch. "It's not so toxic to burn off, and leaves only a slight oily scum on the metal, most of which can be burned off quickly or wiped off with a rag," she writes. If standard red pitch is unavailable, Lansford suggests Northwest Pitchworks' green pitch. "They are equally effective," she writes. "The only advantage I can find in the red is that it seems to become soft at a slightly lower temperature."

<< By Tina Wojtkielo Snyder >>

CLASSIFIED

Subj:

WHY ARTHUR SKURATOWICZ LOVES HIS...
JEWELER'S SAW

SO TELL US. WHAT'S YOUR SECRET WEAPON?

The jeweler's saw. I believe that being able to competently use it enables you to prepare, cut out, detail, and finish just about any jewelry item or component.

WHAT DOES IT DO?

Of course, it's effective at cutting straight lines and complex curves, as well as chaotic shapes. The teeth on the blade also function as a super-micro file, which can crisp up a corner or clean up a prong. As a layout tool, the saw can help with cutting marks for measuring, ensuring symmetry when a mark is transferred from one side of a piece to another—the thin blade behaves like a micro-ruler. And you can use the saw to pre-notch prongs, so you have a starting point before cutting seats.

HOW DO YOU USE IT IN YOUR WORK?

In addition to ring sizing and parts fabrication, I often use the saw to shape and clean up prongs, return corners and details to items I am polishing, and scrape and burnish in tight areas where other tools cannot fit. I can always clean up sloppy filing, cutting, or grinding with my saw.

<103>

WHY DO YOU LOVE IT SO MUCH?

I love the jeweler's saw for its delicate precision; I always check its tautness as a reference point for accuracy. It also enables me to *feel* my progress. I can feel whether I am working with gold, silver, or platinum. I can feel if I cut through to a mounted stone. I can feel when the blade gets dull. I can even feel when things are just not going right. This sensation does not exist with other tools.

WHAT DISCOVERIES OR BREAKTHROUGHS HAVE YOU MADE WITH THIS TOOL?

One thing I've discovered about the jeweler's saw is that it's more accurate than I am, and it's led to a general improvement of my overall ability to work on jewelry. The more I improve my ability to use it, the better it cuts. And the better it cuts, the better able I am to fashion just about anything with it.

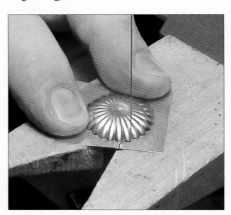

The jeweler's saw is more accurate than I am.

SECRET SHOP TIPS

See, Saw, Saved

Everyone knows jewelers are thrifty, but you'd be amazed at the uses some find for what others would consider trash. Take, for instance, broken saw blades.

"I sometimes use broken saw blades when setting up a piece for soldering," says Judy Stroup of Cleveland, who credits this trick to her teacher, Mary Pangrace. "When you need a part raised just a teeny bit higher, a blade or blades spaced a little bit apart can do the trick." Stack the blades under the piece being soldered to bring the two surfaces level.

"Broken saw blades are good for poking epoxy into half-drilled pearls to set them," reports Brian P. Marshall of Stockton Jewelry Arts School in Stockton, California. "The larger sizes can be used in a pin vise to clean out details in wax models, or sharpened into a very fine 'chisel,' either straight or angled."

Marc Williams of MarcCo Jewelers in Luzerne, Pennsylvania, uses them when he has to do antiquing. "I dip the broken part of a blade in the antique solution and then spread it," he says. "The teeth on the blade help to keep the solution from dripping off."

Broken saw blades have many uses.

"I poke broken saw blades into a firebrick or charcoal block to set up a soldering jig that keeps pieces from moving while they are being soldered," says Frances Gross of Designs by Frances in Dayton, Ohio.

If you're going to use broken saw blades, here's a tip from Amber Gustafson of Amber's Designs in Katy, Texas: "I use a magnet in my bench to keep blades in one place as they break. They really are uncomfortable to accidentally sit on when they fly onto a chair seat!" << **By Suzanne Wade** >>

Subj:

WHY MICHAEL DAVID STURLIN LOVES HIS... GOLDSMITH'S HAMMER

SO TELL US. WHAT'S YOUR SECRET WEAPON?

My goldsmith's hammer.

WHY DO YOU LOVE IT SO MUCH?

I can make an endless body of work with this tool, through the process of forging—pounding directly on the metal.

HOW DO YOU USE IT IN YOUR WORK?

I use the goldsmith's hammer to change the shape and dimension of metal. I can alter the shape from round to square or square to round. I can make the metal tapered, flattened, pointed, curved, domed, arched, thickened, or thinned. I also use this hammer to work-harden the metal as I refine my objects into their final shapes, and to planish, or texture, the surface.

WHAT DOES IT ENABLE YOU TO DO THAT NO OTHER TOOL DOES?

As you strike the metal, you can feel through the hammer how much it's spreading, you can see how much

> As you strike the metal, you can feel how much it's spreading.

it's moving, and you can hear the changes in the metal. There is a very different sound produced when hammering on dead-soft fine silver versus work-hardened fine silver: The sound changes as the metal gets harder. I once tried wearing earplugs when forging; I found it disorienting because I couldn't hear the metal.

WHAT DISCOVERIES OR BREAKTHROUGHS HAVE YOU MADE WITH THIS TOOL?

When I was working on an extensive body of fine-silver forged objects, I had a realization that my use of the hammer in this capacity is actually a direct form of sculpture. Sculpture is

<107>

often perceived as either an additive or a subtractive process, where the material is built up or removed to create a form. In this case, my use of the hammer is a transformative sculptural process. As I direct the metal under the hammer, I change the dimension, shape, form, elevation, surface, and texture of the material; many of these changes are occurring simultaneously. The resulting jewelry objects are thus miniature sculptures—art to be worn and displayed as sculpture. I try to teach this to my students. The first exercise in fundamental goldsmithing is pounding metal with a hammer and seeing what happens. There is so much focus on technology that sometimes we lose sight of creating beautiful jewelry with simple tools. It's the most natural thing we can do.

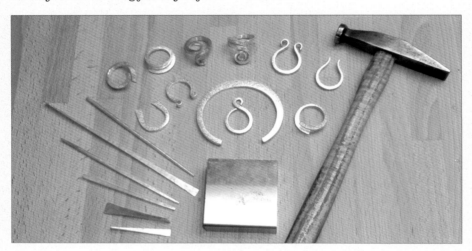

<109>

REGSTR\\DOC SER#032012

SECRET SHOP TIPS

Throw in the Towel

When speaking with bench jewelers about the tools they find most handy, you often hear the usual suspects mentioned: hammers, saws, calipers, gravers, maybe even a laser welder.

Use a good old-fashioned bathroom towel as a bench tool.

But Stephen Fortner, owner of Stephen Fortner Goldsmiths and Fine Jewelry in Victoria, British Columbia, Canada, admits that a good old-fashioned bathroom towel is a mainstay at his bench. It can routinely be found folded up and sitting on top of the open second drawer of his bench, where it makes a great elbow rest. But it doesn't stay there for long, as Fortner puts it to use in many other clever ways.

"When I'm getting ready to set stones, I'll fold the towel in half and lay it flat to cover the bottom of my tray," he says. "If I drop a stone, it won't bounce and always has a soft landing." If you're going to try this, use a colored towel rather than a white one to make fallen diamonds easier to spot.

The towel comes in especially handy when a one-pointer falls out of its mount, or manages to escape the bee's wax as Fortner's bringing the stone to a head. "No more tapping the bottom of my tray, hoping the diamond will bounce up and I can see it," he says.

When his towel isn't doing duty at the bottom of his bench tray, Fortner puts it to work inside his bow pliers when he has to bend a heavy shank. "Any time I want to bend a shank with any of my pliers and I want to make sure I do not leave a mark, I use my towel," he says. "I find it is faster and easier than using tape on my pliers, which just comes off anyway."

So go ahead and throw in the towel. This is one time it could work in your favor. **<< By Shawna Kulpa >>**

Subj:

WHY PATRICIA TSCHETTER LOVES HER...
SPICULUM HAMMERS AND BLOCK

SO TELL US. WHAT'S YOUR SECRET WEAPON?

The Micro Spiculum Hammer, Micro Spiculum Closing Hammer, and Purple Heart Micro Spiculum Block from NC Black Co. LLC.

WHY DO YOU LOVE THEM SO MUCH?

They enable me to make spiculums that are small enough to be used in my jewelry pieces.

HOW DO YOU USE THEM IN YOUR WORK?

I use them to make the spiculums that you see in my "Stem" series of pins/pendants, earrings, and rings. The tools are ideal for working metal from 24 to 30 gauge.

WHAT DISCOVERIES OR BREAKTHROUGHS HAVE YOU MADE WITH THESE TOOLS?

Prior to discovering these amazing tools—which are made by craftspeople for craftspeople—I was making large spiculums that were just too big to use in my jewelry work. With the prices of precious metals reach-ing the stratosphere, I wanted to incorporate hollow forms into my work because they make sense economically. With NC Black's hammers and block, I have made spiculums in 18k pink and yellow gold, 22k yellow gold, silver/22k bi-metal, and Argentium, in sizes ranging from 2 inches long by 1/4 inch in diameter to 7 inches long by 3/8 inch in diameter.

<111>

CLASSIFIED

Subj:

WHY WENDY YOTHERS LOVES HER... RAISING AND PLANISHING HAMMERS

SO TELL US. WHAT'S YOUR SECRET WEAPON?

As a silversmith, I do everything possible with my hammers. There are about 60 well-loved hammers on racks in my apartment, but the ones I cherish the most are my Delrin raising hammer and a planishing hammer that I made 25 years ago.

WHY DO YOU LOVE THEM SO MUCH?

The Delrin hammer is a modern adaptation of the raising hammers I used as a student in Finland and Denmark. Traditional hammers used for the initial forming of metal were made of end-grain ash wood or thick cow's horn. The Scandinavians believed annealed metal raised quicker and work-hardened slower if formed with one of these soft hammers on a steel stake. My Delrin hammer is tougher than ash or horn and does not crack or splinter. Another benefit is that it can be shaped and reshaped as it wears, or as required by the contours of the job at hand. (Wood or horn hammers can be reshaped as well, but they do eventually split and crack.) It's also not as bulky and heavy as the traditional Scandinavian hammers.

My other favorite hammer, the planishing hammer that I made myself, is a beautiful little object. I forged the steel, pierced the hole for the handle, and arrived at the near-completed shape with grinding and filing. I made the apple-wood handle and pre-polished the hammer face with emery cloths and sandpapers ranging from coarse to fine. After achieving a scratch-free surface on the steel and taking it to 400 grit, I polished it on the wheel. I then took the hammer and struck it on a perfectly polished hardened steel anvil. The still-soft hammer face formed gently and incrementally, until it naturally conformed to my careful, measured blows. Work-hardening the face in this way creates a very individual hammer that, when used by

<113>

This tool is an extension of my thoughts.

its maker, seldom makes those awful half-moon marks.

WHAT DO THEY ENABLE YOU TO DO THAT NO OTHER TOOL DOES?

These tools are an extension of my thoughts. I use them to impart the nuances of surface and shape that are only possible with hand hammering.

HOW DO YOU USE THEM IN YOUR WORK?

I never fabricate anything that can be more logically raised, sunk, or spun (i.e., turned or raised on a lathe). Since raising is my method of choice, I use the Delrin hammer to coax a flat sheet into a vessel shape. The planishing hammer comes out after the shape is complete and it's time to perfect the surface.

WHAT DISCOVERIES OR BREAKTHROUGHS HAVE YOU MADE WITH THIS TOOL?

In using my Delrin hammer, I have found that Delrin is also an excellent stake-making material. I have used Delrin to fabricate special stakes for restoration purposes; for example, it comes in very handy when you need to

get a hard-to-reach dent out of a fragile old piece, with no collateral damage. As for my planishing hammer, the act of making it myself taught me patience and instilled in me a great respect for tools, both my own and others'. The work-hardening on an anvil also taught me how to make careful, well-aimed, measured hammer blows, establishing a rhythm that helps me to achieve balance and control when I apply the blows to silver. I think all jewelers and silversmiths should make their own tools, at least once. It's a great learning experience.

<115>

REGSTR\\DOC SER#032012

SECRET SHOP TIPS

If I Had a Hammer

Hammers come in a variety of shapes—but that doesn't mean you have to settle for what's available from the supplier.

For instance, jewelry artist Anne Larsen of Berkeley Springs, West Virginia, found her hammer handle impeding her attempts to master chasing and repoussé. "It was made for a hand bigger than mine, and made to be suitable for either the right or left hand," she says. "Well, I'm a small-handed, right-handed person." Off came the original hammer handle, and Larsen replaced it with a custom-fitted handle that she made.

"I cut out the handle with the scroll saw, put it in a vise, and went file, file, grab, until I had the feeling I wanted," she says. "I learned about the asymmetry of my own closed hands, and I built little facets where my fingers wanted to go."

The results astounded her. "I did some tests, chasing long arcs [with the old

custom-fit a hammer handle for better strikes.

hammer]. Chasing long arcs using a straight tool is one of the hardest things to do," she recalls. "Then I did a series of identical arcs using the new hammer. [The difference] was unbelievable. You don't realize how much steering you need to be able to do with hammer strikes. I never had a secure grip on that [original] handle. I never would have gotten a good strike."

<< By Suzanne Wade >>

<117>

Secret Shop Weapons in Action

In this section, technical editor Ann Cahoon
demonstrates a few "secret weapons" as she
tackles two projects: Creating a fancy-shaped
bezel and crocheting a chain necklace. Videos
of both projects, along with several others
showing various tools in action, are available
on *mjsa.org*; see page 160 for details.

Secret Shop Weapons in Action

CREATING A FANCY-SHAPED BEZEL

SECRET WEAPONS USED:
Miniature stakes
Digital caliper
Jeweler's saw
Hammer

1. Using the digital caliper, I begin by measuring the stone—an asymmetrical trillion—from the table down to the culet. In this case, the distance is nearly 4.5 mm, so I want to make sure I start with about 4.5 to 5 mm of stock, to ensure that the culet is appropriately buried within the bezel. ▼

2. Rather than traditional bezel strip, I like to use thick, rectangular wire, so I have plenty of room to cut a seat. The wire I'm using here is 20 gauge, 5 mm wide by 0.75 mm deep. ▼

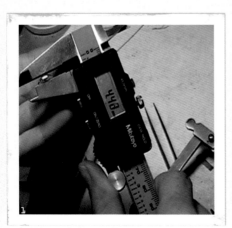

<119>

3. For this particular bezel, I'm going to score and bend the stock to mimic one of the Vs in the stone. (I'll use a second piece of stock for the third wall of the bezel.) Using the digital caliper, I measure the distances between the three corners of the stone. For this stone, the measurements are 10.11 mm... ▼

4. ...6.88 mm... ▼

5. ...and 7.99 mm. The two shorter sides total about 15 mm, but I can't use just that amount of stock: I have to accommodate for the curve in the stone. The

actual scoring and bending will also take up some material. Since we're working in sterling, I'm going to be on the generous side and start with 3 mm of overage, so 18 mm total. (If I were working in gold, I'd have much finer tolerances.) ▼

6. I keep a machinist's ruler in my sweeps drawer. Using it as a gauge, I open out my dividers until they reach a distance of 18 mm. Rather than starting from the end of the ruler, at 0, I find it's much more accurate to start from the 1 and then just subtract 10. ▼

7. Making sure that the end of my stock is fairly straight and flat, I use the dividers to measure and mark off that 18 mm distance on the sterling. ▼

8. Using my jeweler's saw, I cut the stock to length. ▼

9. Again using the machinist's ruler as a gauge, I set the dividers so they'll bisect the 18 mm stock, then mark that distance on the metal. Although this is not a symmetrical stone, 9 mm on either side should be enough to create the shape we need with a little bit of extra

metal, but not so much that we're left with a wasteful mess. ▼

10. Before trying to bend and score the stock, I first anneal it. After applying paste flux, I place the stock on a charcoal surface and heat it with a reducing flame (i.e., the flame contains more gas than oxygen). I especially like charcoal when working with silver, since it adds to the reducing atmosphere and also is naturally reflective, feeding heat back into the piece. Because silver is so conductive, we need a big flame. ▼

<121>

11. I could create this bend by scoring with a saw blade and a file, but in this case I'm going to do it quickly by forging the stock on a miniature stake. I line up that 9 mm layout line with the outside edge of a square-edge stake. ▼

12. I forge straight down, registering the layout line. I hammer both sides, striking in toward that corner. ▼

13. Striking in toward the corner creates a nice, crisp V. Particularly when you're dealing with faceted stones, that crispness is really helpful. ▼

14. Once I have that crisp V, I can adjust the curve of each side to better fit the stone. This can be done by either forging (as I choose to do) or using forming pliers at the bench. ▼

15. I test the fit of the faceted stone—pretty good conformity, for a starting point. We now need to take the stock back to the bench, inspect it, trim the ends, create a curve to cap the stone, and prepare it for finishing. ▼

16. Once I return to the bench, I put on my Optivisor to see whether there are any small areas that need a bit more work. In this case, I see a tiny irregularity on the left side, as well as an unattractive deflection. ▼

17. I could go back to the stake to remove the irregularity, but in the interest of efficiency I'm going to use forming pliers. I'm a big fan of using the bench pin as my third hand. I've found that if you work against the pin, you get just enough non-marring leverage. ▼

18. For the deflection, I'm going to go back to the stake and forge it out. I'm now working over the curved rather than the 90-degree part of this stake, gently adjusting and removing the flat spot. ▼

<123>

19. Such adjustments can make a big difference in quality. In this case, when I'm back at my bench, I can see that it's really improved the shape and conformity of the bezel. ▼

20. Now I want to get the ends trimmed back to accept the third wall of the bezel, which we'll solder into position. Before I do anything else, though, I'm going to stop and anneal the stock. We've done a great deal of forging—here you can see the hammer marks on the surface. ▼

If we don't anneal now, then when we start to solder the assembly and the metal passes through its annealing temperature, the surface could relax a little. We want to relieve any stresses and make sure the bezel's shape will remain as we want it.

21. To anneal, I'm again going to use paste flux and a charcoal block, along with a big reducing flame. The nice thing about paste flux is it creates distinct surface changes that tell the story of how the metal is heating. Rather than looking for subtle color changes, you just have to watch for the surface to change from wet and watery to dry and pasty. And when the flux actually melts and starts to flow, the surface becomes glassy. The flux is a much more accurate indicator of the metal's temperature—especially if you're in a studio that's particularly bright, making it difficult to see subtle colors. ▼

22. After double-checking to make sure we haven't had any unexpected changes in the bezel or how it fits the stone, I'm going to measure the two sides of the stone that will fit into the bent stock. Using my dividers, I measure each side from corner to corner. ▼

23. I then transfer those measurements onto the stock. Centering myself on the metal's ridge, I draw parallel lines. ▼

24. I cut the stock to size, working just outside the layout line. After the cuts are done, I'll file away the excess. ▼

25. As I'm filing the ends, I want to make sure that I'm filing them back, so the points of the stone and the entire girdle will be able to extend about 30 percent to 50 percent into the width of the stock. A lot of jewelers will use a needle file for this because we're working on a fairly fine scale, but I actually prefer a 6-inch hand file. I find that the bigger the tool, the more efficient it is, particularly when I'm trying to keep a surface line straight and square; there's less flex with the larger file. ▼

<125>

26. I'm now ready to add the third wall of the bezel. ▼

27. The severity of the curve or the complexity of the shape will dictate whether you shape the stock by hand or you forge it. Since we're dealing with 20 gauge material and we have a fairly soft curve, I'm just going to do this by hand with forming pliers. ▼

28. Right now I'm not particularly worried about the conformity of the seams; I'm just eyeballing them as I check the fit. Once I have a close fit, I'll file the ends and refine them. ▼

29. I shape the ends while I refine them, adding a bit of curvature so that the two ends of the V will meet up nicely with that third wall. I do bits at a time, periodically checking the fit. ▼

30. A good fit. ▼

32. With my jeweler's saw, I cut away the excess. ▼

31. With my dividers, I scribe a layout line on the third wall, marking where I should cut. I leave a little bit of overage, just to be safe. ▼

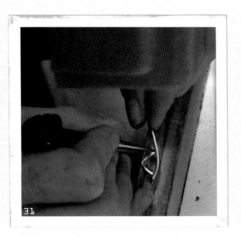

33. With my Optivisor, I double-check the seams to make sure they align correctly. Never undertake a soldering operation without first checking the fit of the seams. ▼

<127>

34. I place solder on each joint and apply heat around the piece. The solder will be drawn into the seams by capillary action, as it follows the torch's heat. ▼

36. I now check the fit. What I want to see is a fairly even bezel edge and good conformity. ▼

35. Before checking the fit, I remove any excess solder. ▼

37. Satisfied with the fit, I trim the ends... ▼

38. ...and smooth the edges. ▼

39. I check one last time to see if there's anything that might interfere with the fit. In this case, I see that a bit of solder is occluding the corner. I use a ball bur to remove it—since it doesn't matter if the inside of the corner is cosmetically square, I don't worry about using the bur rather than a graver. ▼

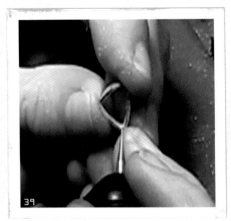

<129>

40. The finished bezel is now ready for the next step, whether that's polishing or modification. ▼

Secret Shop Weapons in Action

CROCHETING A CHAIN NECKLACE

SECRET WEAPONS USED:

Parallel Locking Pliers

Delrin Drawplate

Digital Caliper

Presenter's Note: I used 24 gauge fine silver wire for this project, but you can also do this in sterling, palladium, 14k gold, and 18k gold. I cut the wire into discrete lengths of 18 inches, and since it's a fine gauge I didn't anneal—if I did, the wire would have a tendency to kink more than I'd want for this process.

1. To start, I'm going to use a little bit of a cheat: a scrap of paper. I fold the paper ▼ over a few times, then begin wrap-ping the wire around it. This will determine the number of loops that form the chain's diameter.

2. We're going to start with four loops, for an even number. Three loops are the minimum, but the sky's the limit. ▼

3. I wrap the tail of the wire around itself, just under the loops, creating a "start"; this will not only help to keep the loops organized, but also give me a handle with which to hold the chain as it develops. Note: If you're working in precious metal, you don't want to begin your chain in that material; the start will ultimately be clipped away and discarded, and the lost precious metal

<131>

can quickly add up. Instead, start your chain in sterling or copper, create some foundation rows, then switch to your precious material. ▼

5. In the next step, I bring the wire's tail back up through the center of the loop, so it's where we need it for the crocheting to begin. You can see now why super-long lengths of wire are tricky. ▼

4. I then pull out the loops, organizing them into a flower shape. ▼

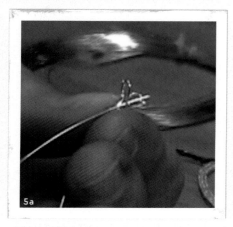

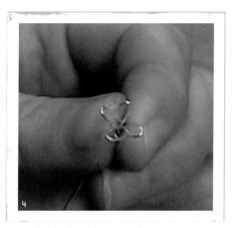

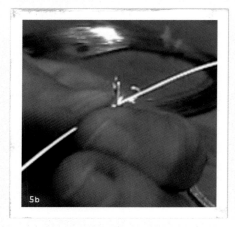

6. We're ready to start the process. ▼

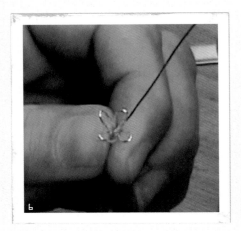

7. The crocheting process requires a mandrel or a tool on which to loop the wire. There are a couple of options. You can use a tapered scribe, which will enable you to create a uniform loop size if you work consistently at the same section of the scribe... ▼

8. ...or you can use a more cylindrical tool. The nice thing about the tapered scribe is that it gives you a bit of flexibility: You can use the same tool for many different loop sizes. ▼

9. The crocheting process is simple. I have the wire I'll be working with coming out from the loop at the 6 o'clock position. ▼

<133>

10. I'm going to take the end of the wire and feed it back through the loop that it came out of... ▼

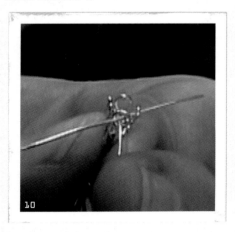

11. ...so that it passes through the loop next door. ▼

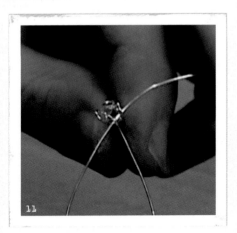

12. I then insert my scribe through the center of the new loop... ▼

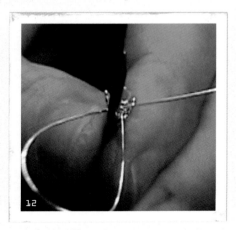

13. ...and pull the wire around the tool, applying firm pressure to create a nice, symmetrical, organized loop. One of the tricks to this process is figuring out how hard to pull. If you pull too hard, you'll deform the loop next door; if you don't pull hard enough, you won't get a nice conformity in your loops. ▼

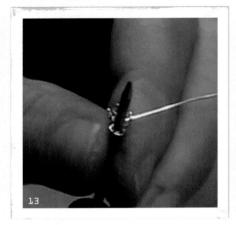

14. I then tip up the loop... ▼

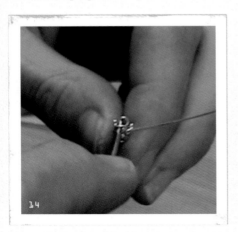

15. ...so that it creates a stitch on top of the one below it. ▼

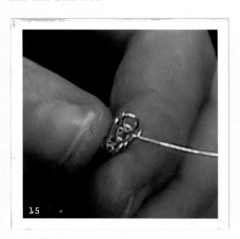

16. I repeat the process with the wire, feeding it back through the loop and out through the neighboring loop. ▼

17. Very quickly, I build up a structure of loops. ▼

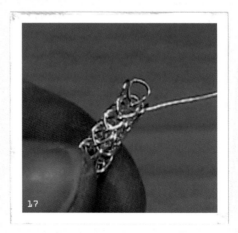

<135>

18. When working on a structure like this, I want to keep it organized as I go along. Because this is hollow, I can actually insert the weaving tool itself into the center of the structure to keep a nice, symmetrical tube. ▼

19. When you come to the end of the wire, you'll need to splice in a new wire to keep going. When it's time to do the splice, the process changes a bit: Instead of feeding the wire back through a loop and out the neighboring loop, I have to feed it back through the loop and up through the center of the structure. ▼

20. Now I need to introduce the new wire. I'm going to bring it in through the neighboring loop, where the previous wire would have continued. ▼

21. As you can see, I'm making a long splice. It's important to make your splice long enough, because if it's too short, it will actually tend to pop out the side of the chain. ▼

22. I twist the two ends together. ▼

23. I've now created about an inch of wound wire, a good starting point. ▼

24. I clip off the ends, and I'm left with a tightly wound splice... ▼

25. ...and another piece of wire with a reasonable working length. ▼

<137>

26. I proceed as I did before, bearing in mind that I now have that splice in the center and have to work around it. I don't want to accidentally capture the splice and pull it to the side of the chain, but instead want to make sure it stays in the center of the structure. Note: This is one of those processes where it's important to wear safety glasses; as the wire end whips about, it's very easy to have it hit your eye—especially since this is a repetitive process and you can easily begin to zone out. ▼

27. When it's time to end the chain, you need to perform the same first step as the splice. Here, I've taken the end and fed it back into the center... ▼

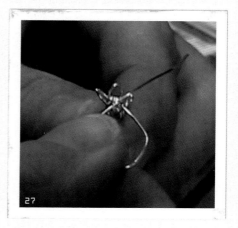

28. ...and pulled the wire tight around the tool point to create a new loop... ▼

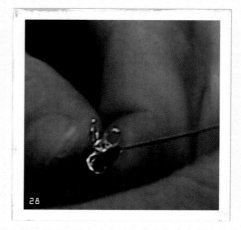

29. ...leaving the end in the center. ▼

30. I'll trim the end back a bit, but not too short or the structure might unwind as I'm doing subsequent steps—think of a run in pantyhose. When the chain is finished, the end cap will cover this. ▼

31. Once the chain reaches the desired length, it's time to anneal and draw. Before annealing, I remove the start, clipping away the links. Since there will be an end cap, I don't need to make the cuts cosmetically perfect; I just need to make sure that little ends don't hang out. Once this is done, I'll anneal the chain to prepare it for drawing. ▼

<139>

32. One way to anneal this is to lay the piece on a clean charcoal block and heat it with a reducing flame (more gas than oxygen). You want to make sure you use a very soft flame, especially with something like 24 gauge material; you don't want to overdo it. I'll know it's ready when I see a subtle shift in color, from shiny silver to frosty white. ▼

33. The chain after quenching. ▼

34. You can also use a trinket kiln, again watching for a slight color change. ▼

35. With crocheted chains, before you draw them, you need to unwind the helix. You can see here how the chain coils during crocheting—the smaller the chain, the tighter the coil. This is just a fact of life, not a concern. ▼

36. Starting at the end, rotate the chain, using thumb and forefinger, to straighten out the row. ▼

37. What you're left with are four straight rows of stitches/loops. Spend a couple of minutes making sure they're truly straight. Don't worry about inconsistencies in loop size; that will be taken care of in the draw. ▼

38. Typically I will double-check the measurement of the chain's outside diameter before I start to draw. You can do this by feel, but it's easy to overdraw quickly if you don't start with a measurement. I use a digital caliper, but you can also use a brass sliding gauge. This chain is about 3.9 mm... ▼

39. ...so I'll do my first draw on the crocheted chain right at 4, then probably go down to 3.5. In this shot you see my personal "secret shop weapon," a Delrin drawplate, which I'll secure in a vise before drawing. ▼

<141>

40. I've taken a piece of 20 gauge copper wire and created a "start" on one end; that will be my handle for drawing the chain through the drawplate. ▼

41. With parallel locking pliers, I pull the chain through the 4 mm hole. (Draw tongs can also be used.) ▼

42. You can see how drawing has quickly regulated and smoothed the chain. ▼

43. It's also increased its flexibility. With these chains, if you work them around a little bit, they get even more supple. ▼

44. Depending on the loop size, you can continue to draw. Here, I draw the chain down again, to 3.5. Be careful not to overdraw, though: It's surprisingly easy to do with these chains, and if you go too far you lose the fluidity. Whenever I'm starting a new style, I make a sample to test how far I can go. ▼

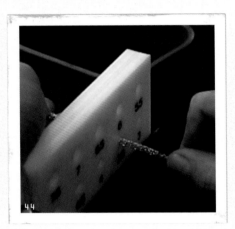

45. You can see how quickly and easily the Delrin draws down the wire and evens it out. ▼

46. Once you remove the copper start and clip off all of the loose ends, the chain is ready for finishing. A polishing wheel is not an option with crocheted chain, which is such a fine structure that buffing drags down the surfaces and leaves them a bit muddy. My preferred methods are to use a brass handbrush to burnish, or to put the chain in a centrifugal pin finishing machine. ▼

<143>

47. When you compare a crocheted chain with a loop-in-loop chain, the difference in the structures is obvious. You can see in the crocheted chain (left) a slightly more open loop, while the loop-in-loop has more of a herringbone effect. Another difference is the way they drape. A loop-in-loop chain is very floppy, while the crocheted chain flexes well but has a bit of bounce. ▼

SECRET
SHOP
WEAP

<145>

Shop Resources

Every jeweler needs a favorite tool—as well as suppliers and other resources through which they can obtain that tool and learn how to put it to best use. The companies, schools, and organizations on the following pages can help.

ORION 150i PULSE ARC WELDER

Your bench space is a precious commodity—so is your time. Adding the Orion 150i Pulse Arc Welder atop your bench will enhance your productivity by giving you the capability to bond metals in ways (and at speeds) not possible with soldering or other arc welders. The best in efficiency and technical capability, the Orion 150i Pulse Arc Welder is your shop's secret weapon for all your welding needs.

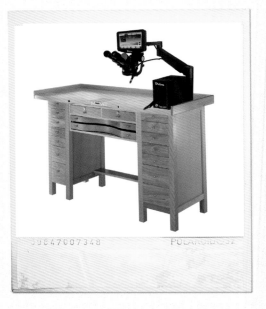

"It's pretty amazing," says Sessin Durgham, awarding-winning jeweler and Rio Grande Technical Support team member. "Jewelers are visual," Sessin says. "The Orion 150i gives me the ability to see where the power level is and what type of arc I'm going to get." The touch-screen display gives you instant control of your weld, allowing you to keep hold of your creation while switching between four weld modes (nano, micro, ultra, and tack) or adjusting power levels. "With the old models, you had to stop working and fiddle with the controls. With the Orion 150i, I can just look up and touch an arrow."

The Orion 150i's microscope provides a built-in shutter that protects your eyes from the flash of the arc. "What you're looking through is a clear, daylight microscope instead of a green screen like other models," says Sessin.

To maximize space and time, Sessin recommends mounting the Orion 150i to your bench and using the swivel arm to swing the welder close to your work or push it away to maximize your workspace.

Call Rio Grande today or visit *riogrande.com* for more information.

7500 Bluewater Road NW
Albuquerque, NM 87121-1962
1-800-545-6566
Fax: 800-965-2329
info@riogrande.com
www.riogrande.com

<147>

BONNY DOON HYDRAULIC PRESS

Take the precision of your favorite hammer and the power of four elephants, merge them into one bench-top tool, and you've got a Bonny Doon hydraulic press.

"It's my 20-ton hammer!" says G. Phil Poirier—inspired designer, metalsmith, engineer, and steward of Bonny Doon Engineering. "The Bonny Doon press gives me incredible power and accuracy. With it, I can form metal easily and with great control—all at the push of a button."

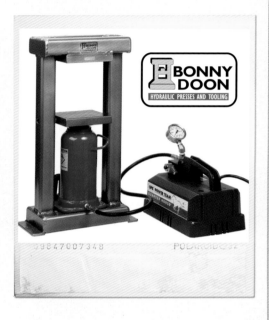

"It's my 20-ton hammer!"

The powerful precision of the Bonny Doon hydraulic press lets you take your designs in creative directions not possible with traditional hand tools.

"Using the Bonny Doon, I'm able to form metals that have already been textured, engraved, embossed, even soldered, without marring or leaving marks," Phil says. "A hammer just can't do that."

Imagine where your creativity will go with the limitless potential of a Bonny Doon hydraulic press.

Visit *riogrande.com* and search "Bonny Doon" for video tips from G. Phil Poirier on the versatility of Bonny Doon. Call Rio Grande today for information on equipping your shop with your own 20-ton hammer.

RIO GRANDE
Since 1944

7500 Bluewater Road NW
Albuquerque, NM 87121-1962
1-800-545-6566
Fax: 800-965-2329
info@riogrande.com
www.riogrande.com

CONTENTI: THE TOOLS OF JEWELERS' DREAMS

All jewelry makers have, at some point, wished for that perfect tool—the one that would make cuts more precisely, or better hold or organize small parts, or help them shape metal more easily. Sometimes they're not even sure such a tool is available—it may exist only in their dreams—but if it were, it would make their lives so much better.

"Excellence consists in the details, the little things," says company president John Contenti. "Oftentimes the realization of those details requires a very particular or specialized tool. Our task, our responsibility, is to have those tools readily available when our customers need them and, where those tools do not yet exist, even to create them. This task is never ending."

Contenti has thousands of innovative products. Contact us for a catalog showing all of our jewelry-making supplies, jeweler's tools, beading supplies, and metalworking tools, or visit us at *contenti.com*. See which tools will fulfill your dreams—and let you rest easier.

Contenti specializes in such tools—the latest, most innovative precision tools and supplies to help jewelers in their pursuit of excellence.

Contenti

515 Narragansett Park Drive
Pawtucket, RI 02861-4323
1-800-343-3364
www.contenti.com

<149>

YOUR MOST IMPORTANT TOOLS AREN'T IN A BOX

It's no secret that an entire production process —filled with creativity, technique and skill—lies between a jewelry designer's imagination and his final piece of work.

Let GIA's Jewelry Manufacturing Arts curriculum take you from idea to reality. You'll learn under the watchful eyes of highly skilled craftsmen and talented instructors who will share their passion and expertise. You'll work in a state-of-the-art classroom at your own fully equipped workbench and learn time-tested techniques and the newest technology.

And you'll earn a professional credential that's recognized world-wide—that's no secret, either.

GESSWEIN: THE RIGHT TOOLS

Established in 1914, Gesswein is an importer and distributor of fine tools, equipment and supplies for jewelry manufacturers and retailers. They feature a comprehensive line of carefully selected, competitively priced items to help your business thrive. Their high-quality items include Galloni casting

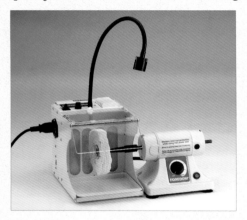

machines, the PUK high-precision arc welder, engravers, polishers, ultrasonics, 3M abrasives, Supra brushes, Quatro dust collectors, and Medalight imaging units. Gesswein carries several micro-motor systems including the Maxima 80, Marathon Handy 700, Mini Mobile

and the Eco-Torque 280, all ideal for grinding, bright cutting and polishing. The Max 24 and Mini Max multi-function finishing machines are great for grinding and polishing. Examples of imaging solutions include the Dino-Lite handheld microscope and the Medalight light boxes. Gesswein is known for unsurpassed customer service, giving the customers more than they expect, responding to their needs immediately, and shipping orders the same day. *Gesswein.com* allows users to see their entire line of products, find current pricing, see the sales and specials, view the tradeshows they will be attending; along with placing orders 24/7.

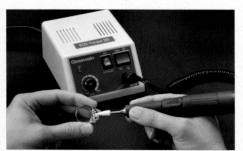

Gesswein®
The Right Tools

201 Hancock Ave.
Bridgeport, CT 06605-0936
1-800-243-4466 or
1-203-366-5400
Fax: 203-366-3953
www.gesswein.com

<151>

BLAINE LEWIS AND NEW APPROACH SCHOOL FOR JEWELERS

Founded in 1996 by Blaine Lewis—widely recognized as the premier diamond setter and platinum-smithing instructor in the U.S.—the New Approach School for Jewelers has always lived up to its name. It emphasizes an innovative, visually intensive alternative to the typical teaching experience: Live demonstrations are projected on large video screens using high-magnification HD cameras, enabling students to see with absolute precision.

"Blaine takes a personal interest in the success of each student, and his work ethic is second to none."

—Michael Kane,
VP of Manufacturing, Tiffany

"The innovative techniques [Blaine Lewis] employs at New Approach put him in front of any school in the nation," says Ross Elliot of Ross Elliot Jewelers in Terre Haute, Indiana.

Now located near Nashville, Tennessee, New Approach continues to inspire, innovate, and train a new generation of jewelers. To learn more, visit us at *new approachschool.com.*

New Approach School for Jewelers
107 Southeast Parkway Court
Franklin, TN 37064-3968
1-800-529-4763 or 1-615-599-3300
blewis@newapproachschool.com
newapproachschool.com

Courses range from five-day power workshops that cover all levels of stone setting (as well as other repair and fabrication fundamentals) to the 12-week Graduate Bench Jeweler Program.

<153>

WHAT CAN RACECAR JEWELRY DO FOR YOU?

If you make your items by hand, you may get to the point where you no longer have the time to do everything yourself. That's when you need to talk with a manufacturer who can explain all the ins and outs of having your designs turned into a reality. You need a company that's able to advise you on how to make the original model, or that can make the model from your designs. You need a company that can produce your models strictly for you, to exacting specifications.

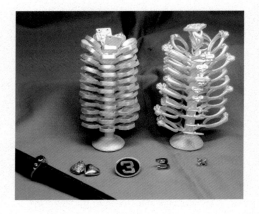

You need RaceCar Jewelry.

Started by Daniel Grandi in 1998 and located in Cranston, Rhode Island, RaceCar is the culmination of Daniel's 38+ years in the jewelry industry. Not only are we committed to providing the finest investment casting manufacturing services available, but using the latest technologies we provide a full range of production services:

Mold making • model making by hand and using CAD/CAM • design consultation • casting • finishing • plating • setting • colored enamels

We can produce raw and finished products in all standard gold colors and karats, all de-ox sterling metals, pink silver, brass, bronze, white bronze, pewter, aluminum, and a form of stainless steel—everything but "unobtainium."

We work very hard to provide the best quality possible for our customers' products, as well as clear information on the production process. In short, what you get at RaceCar is a personal experience. Whether you are casting one piece or 1,000 pieces, we welcome your business. We will work with you to produce your designs the way you want them—and allow you the freedom, time, and energy to develop **new** designs and market your creations.

RaceCar Jewelry Co. Inc.
19 Mendon Ave.
Pawtucket, RI 02861-2335
1-401-461-7803
Fax: 401-270-1196
sales@racecarjewelry.com
www.racecarjewelry.com

SNAG'S FOCUS IS YOU, THE MAKER

People-to-people connections

"SNAG is a wonderful support system for me, while also challenging and enriching my work. I'm a metalsmith not involved with an academic program, and it's great to connect with other SNAG members. We speak the same language."

–*Ginger Meek Allen*

Opportunities

"As a working artist living hand-to-mouth, the SNAG Trunk Show Sale made it possible for me to make my work over the summer rather than get my usual menial summer job."–*Jillian Moore*

Creative inspiration

"*Metalsmith* has it all—beautiful metal jewelry and interesting articles. It inspires me and I share it with newbies who are hungry to stretch their minds and viewpoints."–*Karen Christians*

No-nonsense business advice

"I've formed relationships with members whose knowledge has helped me grow. I've definitely gotten better at how I present my work."

–*Michelle Pajak-Reynolds*

SNAG provides what you need most.

Society of North American Goldsmiths

SN AG FOUNDED 1969

Artists. Designers. Jewelers. Metalsmiths.

540 Oak St., Suite A
Eugene, OR 97401-2674
1-541-345-5689
info@snagmetalsmith.org
www.snagmetalsmith.org

<155>

MYRON TOBACK INC.:
YOUR LINK TO SUCCESS

No matter what type of bench work you do, whether stringing beads or soldering earring posts, at some point you're going to need component parts. And when you do, Myron Toback Inc. will be there to help.

Based on New York City's famed 47th Street, Myron Toback Inc. has been supplying jewelry findings and other supplies for half a century, and jewelers know that they can rely on the company to fulfill even their rarest requests. "We're known for supplying all types of needs, from hard-to-find findings and chain styles to silver hoops and 24k lobster claws to 22k ear posts. We can even personalize findings," says president Michael Toback. He also notes the company's renowned customer service, a reputation for which has been building since his father, Myron, first founded the company in 1963. Word of mouth goes a long way, and more than one jeweler has been told by a colleague, "Go to Myron Toback—they'll treat you well, and they probably stock exactly what you need."

Myron Toback also meets jewelers' needs for tools and supplies, including a full line of both opaque and transparent enamels as well as pure gold, silver, platinum, palladium, and many different alloys of gold: pink, white, green, and yellow. In addition, they offer in-house refining services for any type of scrap—performed, as always, with impeccable customer service.

To place an order, visit *myrontoback .com* to see a complete catalog, or visit them in their New York showroom.

 Myron Toback Inc.

25 W. 47th St.
New York, NY 10036-2875
1-800-223-7550 or
1-212-398-8300
Fax: 212-869-0808
sales@myrontoback.com
www.myrontoback.com

The Contributors

Belle Brooke Barer
Belle Brooke Designs Inc.
Boulder, Colorado
bellebrooke.net

Jim Binnion
James Binnion Metal Arts
Bellingham, Washington
mokume-gane.com

Michael Bondanza
Michael Bondanza Inc.
New York, New York
michaelbondanza.com

Ann Cahoon
Flying Marquis Studio
Pawtucket, Rhode Island
flyingmarquis.com

Gary Dawson
Gary Dawson Designs
Eugene, Oregon
garydawsondesigns.com

John de Rosier
Albany, New York
johnderosier.com

Kathleen DiResta
K. DiResta Design Inc.
Sea Cliff, New York
kdirestadesign.com

Jason Dow
Jason Dow Jewelry Inc.
Honolulu, Hawaii
jasondow.com

Christopher Duquet
Christopher Duquet Fine
     Jewelry Design LLC
Evanston, Illinois
christopherduquet.com

Cynthia Eid
Cynthia Eid Designs
Lexington, Massachusetts
cynthiaeid.com

Geoffrey D. Giles
Geoffrey D. Giles Jewelry
Asheville, North Carolina
geoffreydgiles.com

Brett Gober
Freedom Design & Contracting
Hannibal, Missouri
classicrings.com

Sarah Graham
Sarah Graham Metalsmithing
San Francisco, California
sarahgraham.com

Alishan Halebian
Alishan
Irvine, California
alishanonline.com

Barbara Heinrich
Barbara Heinrich Studio
Rochester, New York
barbaraheinrichstudio.com

Charlie Herner
Green Lake Jewelry Works
Seattle, Washington
greenlakejewelry.com

<157>

Lisa Krikawa
Krikawa Jewelry Designs
Tucson, Arizona
krikawa.com

Lee Krombholz
Krombholz Jewelers/
   Just Like You Designs
Cincinnati, Ohio
justlikeyoudesigns.com

Blaine Lewis
New Approach School for Jewelers
Franklin, Tennessee
newapproachschool.com

Eva Martin
Eva Martin Jewelry
Boston, Massachusetts
evamartin.com

Mark Maxwell
Gemological Institute
   of America (GIA)
Carlsbad, California
gia.edu

Joel McFadden
JMD Jewelry
Red Bank, New Jersey
jmdjewelry.com

Michelle Pajak-Reynolds
Michelle Pajak-Reynolds Studios LLC
Stow, Ohio
michellepajakreynolds.com

Chris Ploof
Chris Ploof Designs Inc.
Pawtucket, Rhode Island
chrisploof.com

Todd Reed
Todd Reed Inc.
Boulder, Colorado
toddreed.com

Alan Revere
Revere Academy of Jewelry Arts
San Francisco, California
revereacademy.com

Corrie Silvia
Cranston, Rhode Island
corriesilvia@hotmail.com

Arthur Skuratowicz
The Jewelry Training Center
Colorado Springs, Colorado
jewelrytrainingcenter.com

Michael David Sturlin
Michael Sturlin Studio
Scottsdale, Arizona
michaelsturlinstudio.com

Patricia Tschetter
Tschetter Studio
Dallas, Texas
tschetterstudio.com

Wendy Yothers
Wendy Yothers Designs
Keaau, Hawaii
wyothers@hawaii.edu

About the Technical Editors

Ann Cahoon, the owner of Flying Marquis Studio in Pawtucket, Rhode Island, is a designer/goldsmith focusing on custom and limited production work in gold and platinum. A graduate of the Maine College of Art and Boston's North Bennet Street School, she is also an instructor at the Metalwerx School for Jewelry and Metal Arts. Her articles appear periodically in *MJSA Journal.*

Chris Ploof is the owner of Chris Ploof Designs Inc. in Pawtucket, Rhode Island. He specializes in original wedding bands and custom jewelry, many of which feature such eclectic materials as meteorite iron, Damascus stainless steel, and mokumé gane. He was named a JCK Las Vegas "Rising Star" in 2010 and is a two-time recipient of the Santa Fe Symposium Industry Leader Award. Chris also serves as a technical consultant to the jewelry industry.

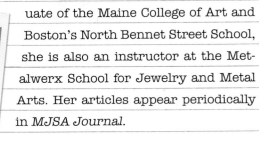

<159>

Index to "Secret Shop Weapon" Tools

See the Secret Shop Weapons in Action on MJSA Online

View exclusive videos and slideshows in which technical editors Ann Cahoon and Chris Ploof, among others, perform various projects with the help of a few "secret shop weapons." You can also submit your own favorite tool and describe the difference it's made in your work. Just go to *mjsa.org/secret_shop_weapons* and enter the custom MJSA member ID and password below. (Please note that the member ID and password will provide access only to the Secret Shop Weapons videos.)

Member ID: 43130
Password: ssw_reader